Spirit Possession

Spirit Possession

The Counterfeit With Many Faces

T. E. Wade, M.D.

with co-authors
Glen Gessele
and
Rick Howard

Gazelle Publications
11560 Red Bud Trail
Berrien Springs, MI 49103

Gazelle Publications
Auburn, California 95603

Copyright © 1991 by
Gazelle Publications, 5580 Stanley Dr., Auburn CA 95603.
All rights reserved.

Edited by Theodore E. Wade, Jr.
Cover art by William Boddy

Scripture quotations are from the New Revised Standard Version of the Bible,
copyright 1989 by the Division of Christian Education of the National
Council of the Churches of Christ in the USA. Used by permission.

Library of Congress Catalog Card Number: 90-81513.
International Standard Book Number: 0-930192-24-9.
Printed in the United States of America.

Contents

Foreword, 9

Viewpoint, 11
*Approach; Possession—unscientific but not antiscientific;
Not a new issue; Insights into the unseen; Ideas to be
shared.*

Encounter with hypnotism, 16
*Curiosity; An unexpected jolt; A stabilizing factor;
Investigation required; Further exploration.*

Awareness, 22
*Awareness and hypnosis; The brain at work; Mental
concentration; Control center; The complexity of
awareness; Simulated awareness.*

Suggestibility, 28
*Leader and subordinate; Suggestion and suggestibility;
Normal response to suggestion; Conversion and the
limits of normal suggestion.*

Hypnosis, 31
*Discrimination; Definition; Characteristics of hypnosis;
How hypnosis is induced; Conditions resembling
hypnosis; A delusion of the last days.*

more - - - >

Possession, 38

> Definition; Communication; Possession a mystery; Possession by the Holy Spirit; . . . by an unholy spirit; Unclean spirits mentioned in Scripture; Spiritism; Transcendental meditation; Double occupancy; Possession and hypnosis; Glossolalia; Glossolalia at Corinth; Possession summarized; Ellen White, possession and hypnosis.

Evil spirit control, 54

> A matter of choice; Sandy's encounter with evil.

The greater power, by Glen Gessele, 57

> Commitment to Satan; Enchanting symbols and music; Problems unresolved; Unwillingness to yield to the Holy Spirit; The Exorcist; Victory in Christ.

Deliverance, 64

> Bondage of sin; Diagnosis; The mind and sanctification; Treatment; Dangers of the deliverance ministry; Success or failure.

In the church, by Rick Howard, 72

> Spiritualism in many forms; Evil angels in control; Visualization; The corridor; Seeking spiritual growth by altered consciousness; Guided meditation; The easy way.

Will and salvation, 79

The will and the two kinds of possession; Perfect will; Will and eternal life; Law; Sin; Atonement; Sanctification; Justification; Salvation.

Conquering, 85

Surrender to Christ is freedom; Hypnosis and conquering.

Impending deception, 90

Revival of sorcery and Satanic deception; A mental picture.

The choice is ours, 95

The only safety from deception.

Careful reading of Dr. Wade's comments about spirit possession clearly reveals the contrast between possession by the Holy Spirit with commitment to the Lord Jesus on the one hand, and surrender to Satan on the other.

I have noted in particular, reference to two youths who were involved with spirit possession. Their experiences took place while I was chairman of the Board of Trustees of the Christian boarding school they were attending. Pastor Glen Gessele was then chaplain of the student body.

I remember the concern of the students as they began to realize that possession by the evil one means losing control of self. Greatly sobered by what they had seen, most of them made a conscious choice to fix their loyalty on the side of Christ the Lord. They understood more forcefully their responsibility for the right use of the will.

The logical reasoning set forth in this book is worthy of serious consideration. Each individual must choose to yield the will to Christ or to domination by the evil one. True happiness comes only through a firm decision to follow the Lord Jesus who lived on earth and died on the cross to assure our eternal freedom.

S. S. Will

Viewpoint

Satan didn't invent spirit possession. His control of those who yield to him is only a takeover of God's throne in their hearts. The abiding relationship Jesus offers—the oneness with Him—is the kind of possession God planned for our happiness from the beginning. "Do you not know," wrote Paul, "that your body is a temple of the Holy Spirit within you"? (1 Cor. 6:19).

Because Satan's kind of control is so different from God's, we may not recognize that it involves the very capacity designed for communion with the Holy Spirit. As we accept union with Christ, fulfilling His will becomes our own purpose and greatest joy. Complete possession is then complete freedom.

Approach

In this book, we consider what it means to be possessed by the Holy Spirit and suggest how the natural mechanism has been misused. Examining the process of hypnosis leads us to notice the similarity between persons under its influence and those possessed by evil spirits. Looking at the mysteries of the nervous system helps us visualize how such a phenomenon as hypnosis might occur. We discuss the meaning of deliverance from evil spirit control. And finally, we consider how yielding to the control of either the Holy Spirit or the enemy of souls could relate to the last great struggle between good and evil before our Lord returns.

Possession—unscientific but not antiscientific

Some would like to believe in a gracious, orderly God, but their educational experience imposes doubts. They question the reality of angels, the devil and creation because science cannot demonstrate or prove them.

We here use the term *metaphysics* in its broader sense, not confining it to quasi-religious, crystal-ball type phenomena that often come to mind. Some people, who feel unable to accept the possible reality of anything science cannot explain, view metaphysical concepts with contempt. The word metaphysics means beside or outside of physics. *Physics,* in its original meaning, is the knowledge or understanding of nature based on observation. Today the term *empirical science* expresses that meaning.

To illustrate knowledge based on observation, we may say that all swans are white because we have seen many white swans. As we see more and more white swans, our confidence in that assertion increases until we conclude that it is really true. However, finding even one black swan would disprove the assertion making it no longer acceptable. In the meantime, until we find a swan that is not white, we consider this statement to be scientifically true.

Thus our confidence in a scientific theory depends on its ability to survive tests which could show it to be false. By contrast, metaphysical concepts lay no claim to verification by scientific testing, and therefore require other means to establish their credibility.

With these definitions in mind, notice comments by the eminent scientist, Sir Karl Raimund Popper. The basic principle he sets forth is relevant to our problem.

"I do not even go so far as to assert that metaphysics has no value for empirical science. . . . I am inclined to think that scientific discovery is impossible without faith in ideas which are of a purely speculative kind, and sometimes even quite hazy; a faith which is completely unwarranted from the view of science, and which to that extent, is 'metaphysical.'" [1]

I can suggest no test that would prove my belief in God, as Creator and Sustainer, to be wrong. God cannot be analyzed experimentally. My belief is based on experience. As I observe the intricate and obviously purposeful design in the structure and function of living things, I am compelled to believe that there must be a designer.

Although the Bible was written and copied over many centuries, still its central message seems so reasonable and consistent, that my attention is carried beyond the human writers to the divine Author Who has inspired and preserved it. Observing the fulfillment of prophecy strengthens my confidence that the Holy Scriptures contain God's counsel for me.

Now what about the alternative concept, atheism? Its adherents consider belief in a metaphysical Creator to be beneath the dignity of any intelligent person in this modern age of empirical science. Atheism, they seem to feel, is self-evident. But, since no test has been devised which, if applied, could show it to be incorrect, that concept also is metaphysical, not empirical!

Now you may say, "So what? You haven't proved anything." I heartily agree. In fact, that is just the point. Not all ideas, including many in this book, can be proved or disproved. Fundamental beliefs may rest on evidence beyond the scope of scientific verification.

Not a new issue

Roughly 500 years before Christ, Hippocrates, on the Greek island of Cos, began to teach that illness resulted from understandable abnormalities of body tissues or fluids. Physicians of the Hippocratic school attributed psychosis to brain disease.

Since Hippocrates' day, understanding has improved in both science and religion. Brain disease is better understood, and people in our society do not worship capricious gods. But contention between self-confident medical scientists and earnest religionists still arises concerning the proper treatment of mental disorders. Rigid dogmatism on the part of either side is unjustified.

Edwin Yamauchi, from the history department at Miami University, has surveyed the literature on this topic as it relates to the miracles of Jesus. His final paragraph is worth noting:

"Who can say that chemical possession by drugs such as heroin and cocaine in the western world is any less destructive or diabolical than demonic possession? The enduring message of the Gospel is that Christ died and rose to triumph over all principalities and powers, and that He can deliver us from all demons and obsessions, whether chemical or psychological or spiritual."[2]

Insights into the unseen

One of the many authors we quote in these pages deserves a special explanation: Ellen White wrote on spiritual topics mostly in the latter half of the nineteenth century and has had a profound influence on the development of the Seventh-day Adventist Church. In the next chapter, I explain how my early reservations about her ministry developed into confidence. Even if you happen to disagree with my personal convictions, I believe you will find her insights helpful as we look at the spiritual dimension of mind manipulation.

Ideas to be shared

This book has taken shape slowly, urged on by ideas that refuse to die. Various professors, physicians, editors, pastors and my own two sons have encouraged, advised, provided source material and edited this work. I have written to share my joy of knowing God as revealed in Christ and communicated through His indwelling Spirit.

It is my prayer that, as you read these pages, the Holy

14

Spirit may guide your understanding of issues often obscured in our modern world.

References

1. Karl R. Popper, *The Logic of Scientific Discovery*. Harper Torchbooks, Harper and Row, Publishers, New York 1968, p. 38.

2. Edwin Yamauchi, *Gospel Perspectives, Volume 6, The Miracles of Jesus*. JSOT Press, Dept. of Biblical Studies, Sheffield S1O 2TN, England, 1986, p. 149.

Encounter

A magician was to appear in town! He announced that he would saw a woman in two and put her back together. He would pull rabbits from a hat and he would hypnotize volunteers from the audience. My nine-year-old mind was thrilled. But my father saw matters otherwise. Hypnosis, he explained, was of the devil. No child of God would attend such a meeting, and that was that.

Curiosity smoldered through my years of high school, college, medical school and into early medical practice. Then, at Moses Lake (Washington) Army Air Base, during World War II, I encountered hypnotism in practice. The base psychiatrist had been trying to help bed-wetting airmen. At a hospital staff meeting, he discussed the problem and demonstrated some of his methods.

An unexpected jolt

The psychiatrist hoped that the bed wetters could be helped by deep hypnotic suggestion. He demonstrated the induction of hypnosis and some of its classical manifestations. One by one, five airmen, who had been repeatedly hypnotized, were presented to the medical staff. As each airman came into the room, he was told that we were doctors who desired to help him, and that he need not be afraid.

The first airman was hypnotized. He was asked to lie on three chairs arranged side by side. Then he was told that the center chair would be removed, but his body would not sag and that he would feel no fatigue. The center chair was removed. The young man remained motionless while the officer discussed the progress of his project. Then the chair was replaced under the man's hips and he was asked to stand. When asked whether lying on the chairs had been difficult he said it had not.

After hypnotizing the second airman, the psychiatrist handed him a large, heavy book, and asked him to hold it above his head with one hand. The soldier did this, seemingly with ease, for perhaps ten minutes. While holding the book, he was asked to turn the pages with his free hand. When the experiment was over, the soldier said he felt no fatigue and was dismissed.

The psychiatrist hypnotized the third airman. Then he began introducing him to each of the doctors present. However, at two vacant chairs he introduced the young man to doctors who were absent. I was passed by without an introduction.

When asked to identify the doctors, he pointed and counted, including the two fictitious persons and completely ignored me. Then, pointing to me, the psychiatrist asked, "Did you miss the man in this chair?" The young man looked straight at me and replied, "That chair is empty, Sir." After being released from the trance, he appeared surprised to see me sitting in front of him.

A fourth airman was hypnotized and told that he would stand motionless without breathing. A lighted candle held close to his face burned without a flicker. We were told that he did actually breathe but in a very gentle, controlled manner.

When the fifth airman had been hypnotized, his hand was cleansed with alcohol, which he was told would make it numb. A needle was pushed into the flesh and he did not flinch. He denied any feeling of pain.

These experiments demonstrated four types of hypnotic response. The man who lay suspended between two chairs, and the man who held the large book, both experienced catatonia. In this state, the individual maintains his posture like a living statue. Catatonia is also seen in certain severe mental disorders. However, in hypnosis it may be induced without mental disease.

The soldier who saw two persons not present, but who failed to see me, demonstrated both positive and negative hallucination. Later, we will examine this phenomenon in more detail.

The soldier who did not seem to breathe demonstrated so-called *suspended animation*. The man who felt no pain demonstrated *hypnotic anesthesia*.

I should point out that showmanship of this type is rarely, if ever, used clinically.

I left that meeting deep in thought. For several years I had felt perplexed by questions about Ellen White and her work. A friend had chided me, "You Adventists quote everything that Ellen White ever wrote or said. You allow her to mold your doctrine. You seem to think her pen was infallible." Frankly, I sympathized with these feelings. In fact, a few of her comments, I felt, did not harmonize with logic or with known scientific "fact."

Since my youth, I had heard about Ellen White's physical conditions during vision which I had accepted as evidence of divine inspiration. But this army psychiatrist, using hypnosis, had apparently duplicated some of these very phenomena.

A seemingly inevitable question confronted me. "Were Seventh-day Adventists deceived by a pious, dynamic person who sincerely believed that she spoke for the Lord, but who, in fact, was the victim of hypnosis?"

A stabilizing factor

My confidence in the prophetic gift has been influenced by experiences of my parents when I was a child. After receiving a letter from Ellen White, my father abandoned his plan to build a sanitarium at a hot-water artesian well near Cañon City, Colorado. But the project remained dear to his heart; and a number of years later, when he tried again at another site, the project died before taking its first breath.

I was nearly of age when my mother told me of the special counsel they had received. She had been impressed that Mrs. White, who did not know my father, had accurately described his personality. He had been warned that the enterprise would not succeed and that persistence would jeopardize his soul salvation.

More than sixty years after the counsel was given, I had the privilege of visiting the White Estate vault and reading one of the letters which he had received. Time had demonstrated the accuracy of her advice.

Investigation required

I had always supported the idea of the modern gift of prophecy, but at the time I encountered the hypnosis demonstration, my knowledge of Ellen White's work had been based on hearsay and on brief quotations I had read or heard. Occasionally I had examined the index of her writings to find support for an idea. A few times I had read an entire chapter from one of her books, which I considered boring.

Now it was time to take a closer look—to establish confidence. Although I did not tell my wife why I wanted to study Ellen White's writings more thoroughly, she readily agreed to my suggestion. Each morning we read half a dozen pages from one of Ellen White's books until we had completed it. Then we read another book and another until we had read nearly all. We began with *Early Writings*. Then we read *The Ministry of Healing, The Conflict of the Ages* series, *Testimonies for the Church,* and other books. This habit proved so rewarding that we continue it to this day. Some of those books we have read several times.

At one time, someone had suggested that Ellen White's comments and personal opinions should be considered less authoritative than her visions. At first, as we read, I watched for clues to identify more and less inspired statements. However, all seemed consistent. No separation could be made. As we continued, confidence increased. With the passing of years, one after another of the statements which had seemed questionable or incompatible with scientific observation, proved to be correct. There still remain a few statements that I cannot harmonize with my background of ideas, just as there are a few verses in the Bible which seem illogical, but these comprise such a small fraction of the whole that they are of no consequence. With increased understanding, even these may resolve themselves. And, after all, has God asked me to be the standard of absolute truth?

To me, the writings of Ellen White inspire confidence in the Scriptures. They present an all-wise, loving heavenly Father, and a Saviour whom I can love and trust. I do not let a few imponderable questions blind my mind to the over-whelming evidence that God lives, and that He speaks to us through His prophets.

God saw fit to demonstrate phenomenal physical conditions in Ellen White during her visions, especially in her early ministry. Thus acceptance was established. However, since miracles can be imitated (See Exodus 9), it is within the messages themselves and in their harmony with Scripture that the believer today must find evidence that they deserve confidence. This was the conclusion my wife and I derived from reading and studying Ellen White's writings.

Further exploration

I am naturally curious. Though the phenomena demonstrated at the army staff meeting did not lead me to reject the work of Ellen White, I could not help but wonder where the relationship might lie. Since then I have given much thought to the question of hypnosis, particularly as it relates to the question that confronted me so abruptly during my military service.

We have been advised against involvement in hypnosis, but should it be ignored? If we lived in snake infested country, we would not unnecessarily expose ourselves to poisonous reptiles, but we would learn enough about snakes to avoid injury.

To human wisdom, a fuzzy line often separates truth from error. In fact, they seem to intermingle at some points. We have been told, "The Word of God is quick, and powerful, and sharper than any two-edged sword, piercing even to the dividing asunder of soul and spirit, and of the joints and marrow, and is a discerner of the thoughts and intents of the heart" (Heb. 4:12, KJV). To a student of anatomy this metaphor is very meaningful. Marrow is a fragile, blood-producing tissue protected within bone. Along the central length of a bone, any child can easily separate the marrow from the bone, but as one approaches the joint, spicules of bone become so intimately interspersed with the marrow that separation becomes practically impossible. Similarly only the wisdom of God's Word can separate truth from error.

Normal response to suggestion is easily differentiated from deep hypnotic trance. However, the unavoidable fringe areas call for deeper study into God's Word through the guidance of His Holy Spirit. The chapters which follow reveal conclusions drawn from my study and are recorded for anyone who feels challenged by these problems.

Hypnosis distorts discrimination, appreciation and evaluation. And these functions are inseparably related to awareness, which we look at in the next chapter as we begin our study of hypnosis and possession.

Awarencess

Awareness is consciousness of conditions, persons, or ideas. Awareness may be genuine or distorted. It may be real or fictitious. It may be vague or vivid. By hypnotic suggestion awareness may be induced, altered, or obliterated. Because awareness and hence discrimination are profoundly affected by the hypnotic trance, the phenomenon is of great interest to the person who feels accountable to God. How awareness might be distorted is intriguing. Perhaps interference with some kind of selective switching mechanism in the brain produces hypnotic suggestion and spirit possession. Fatigue of such a mechanism might explain hysteria. And indeed, study of the brain reveals junctions with selective switching capacity at every point where nerve cells communicate or contact each other. Discussing the brain's function in more detail will make it easier to visualize what might happen to influence awareness.

The brain at work

Mystery surrounds the very nature of the thought process. However, we do have a few clues. In the brain's superficial gray layer, or *cortex,* are billions of interconnecting nerve cells called *neurons.* Each neuron has connections or *synapses* permitting it to receive electrochemical signals from hundreds of other neurons. In addition, it can transmit signals to one or another or to many other neurons. The neuron does not forward every signal but in some way controls which signals to send on and which cells should receive them. A neuron acts within a thousandth of a second either passing on or blocking a particular signal. The receiving cell may be adjacent or at a considerable distance from the sending cell. Waves or streamlets of electrochemical activity flow through the cortical substance more or less constantly. The wave front may affect hundreds of nerve cells at one time, and may flow through a million of them within one second. Dozens of these waves or streamlets are flowing simultaneously, intersecting each other. At any moment in time, some spots in the brain cortex are electrochemically active while others are quiescent. This complex interplay is probably the basis of mental activity. Some have compared the brain to a gigantic computer.

Mental concentration

The mind can give keen attention to only one thing at a time. To avoid confusion it is equipped to eliminate, suppress, or relegate to a subconscious level, everything else. Distortion and exaggeration of this function may explain the abnormal awareness of hypnosis, to be discussed in a later chapter. For those who care to know, we will mention the mechanism which apparently makes mental concentration possible. Then we will illustrate normal awareness by citing two examples.

Control center

We have described the action of the individual neuron which resembles a minute electronic relay with discriminating ability. In addition, a specialized area of the brain has been identified which seems to have the purpose of arousing and alerting the cerebral cortex. Evidently it sorts and evaluates incoming signals according to significance and controls their flow from one brain area to another. This control center, called the reticular formation, is about the size of a little finger and is located in the brain stem. Our awareness of the world and our ability to think, to learn, and to act depend on it. Without it an individual would be unconscious and paralyzed. Thinking, perception and intelligent response to stimulus, center in the cortex of the brain. To function, the cortex must be aroused.

In other words, "Concentration, reality testing, and simple survival require the exercise of scanning and screening mechanisms to keep the searchlight of awareness focused on selected areas of psychic content and to keep everything else out of awareness."[1]

This reticular activating system (or RAS) "awakens the brain to consciousness and keeps it alert; it directs the traffic of messages in the nervous system; it monitors the myriads of stimuli that beat upon our senses, accepting what we need to perceive and rejecting what is irrelevant; it tempers and refines our muscular activity and bodily movements. We can go even further and say that it contributes in an important way to the highest mental processes—the focusing of attention, introspection and doubtless all forms of reasoning."[2]

"In short, the RAS acts as a kind of traffic control center, facilitating the flow of signals in the nervous system."[3]

The vast majority of signals sent to the brain from all over the body are suppressed. For instance, no person is aware at every moment of every part of his skin; but if he happens to sit on a pin he suddenly becomes acutely aware of the signal sent up by the spot which the pin pricks. Even a strong signal may not reach consciousness until the brain is prepared for it. If a person accidentally smashes his finger, he may experience no pain for a moment. Very soon, however, the matter will catch his attention and he will be aware of pain. By contrast if a knife were held over his finger and slowly pressed down his suffering would be intolerable. Thus we see some of the factors which influence normal awareness.

The complexity of awareness

Awareness is a very complex process. It involves the normal senses such as touch and sound as well as the brain's ability to organize and interpret the messages it receives.

As an example of the sorting process, let us examine the

sense of sight. The eye resembles a camera. The retina, corresponding to the camera film, contains microscopic light-sensitive nerve cells. When a unit of light strikes one of these cells, a chemical change takes place that sends out a signal. Deep in the retina are three successive nerve cell groups through which the signal must pass. Cells in each of these groups either reject the signal or accept it and direct its continuation. From the retina signals are carried by fibers of the optic nerve to the midbrain where they are screened again by the reticular formation before they reach the visual area in the back of the brain. Sight becomes part of awareness as the combined optic signals are compared with information being received from other sensory mechanisms and with that stored in the memory. The imagination evaluates the significance of this visual information and its probable effect on the person.

All of this happens in a fraction of a second. The eye receives hundreds of thousands of light units simultaneously. The brain does not sense each of these separately. Rather all the lights and darks, the spots of color and the shapes are combined and compared with information stored from previous experience to produce one composite picture. Thus in a flash one knows whether an object he encounters is a snake or a dog, whether it is his wife or a neighbor. He knows whether she is happy or angry, and he decides whether to be joyful, sad or alarmed. All of this is what we call awareness. And it is far more complex than our imagination can grasp. The point to be noted is that sorting, evaluation and discrimination are involved at every step of the process.

Simulated awareness

Just as the brain can block authentic signals, so it can generate signals that seem to be real. Imagination is the ability to perceive in the mind that which is not present to the senses. A combination of imagination and memory can produce simulated awareness. Thus wherever a person may be, he knows what his house is like inside and out. He can picture how a new chair will affect the decor of the living room. Simulated awareness is normal if the person realizes that it is simulated and unreal.

Psychotic individuals, however, may be unable to distinguish between the real world on the outside and the imaginary world within their minds. Fantasies are often very real to children. Dreams are products of the imagination which the sleeping person is normally unable to distinguish from reality.

As obvious examples of fictitious awareness, consider the false sensation of light caused by pressing the side of a closed eye, or the constant ringing some people hear when there is no sound.

Now suppose a sensation or an idea is inserted into the thought pathway, by suggestion. And suppose this occurs while one's discrimination and evaluation capacity are depressed or obliterated by hypnosis. We can easily see how this suggestion or idea might be accepted as reality. The inability to distinguish between reality and imagination while one is awake we know as hallucination. Positive abnormal awareness (the condition of hallucination) requires input from the imagination, and probably from memory. The imagination inserts images into the cerebral pathways, and the subject becomes aware of these as though they were truly present.

Conversely, negative distortion of awareness occurs when legitimate information is blocked. Our ability to concentrate on a chosen topic requires selectively suppressing irrelevant sensory input. But overaction of this suppressive mechanism can produce distortion by obliterating certain areas of awareness.

Consider, as an example, the devout Hindu who walks on hot coals, or thrusts a large needle through his cheek. By denial of reality he can block his sensory mechanism and thus endure without flinching an experience that most of us would find intolerable.

Awareness is perception of a situation, a state of being, or a presence. Its intensity may vary. Thus awareness may be a vague impression, or it may be so strong that it crowds all else from the mind. Awareness may be focused by being called to a person's attention, or it may be suppressed by diverting the thoughts. Awareness may be genuinely accurate, or it may be illusionary.

Hypnosis manipulates awareness.

References

1. Louis J. West, M.D., "Psychophysiology of Hypnosis," *Journal of the American Medical Association,* Feb. 13, 1960, Vol. 172, p. 672. Copyright 1960, American Medical Association.

2. J. D. French, *Scientific American,* May, 1957. Reprinted in *Altered States of Awareness,* pp. 29ff, 1972 W. H. Freeman & Co., New York.

3. *Ibid,* p. 29.

Suggestibility

Next we consider suggestibility, an area where underbrush may make the trail more difficult to follow. Like awareness, suggestibility is an element of day by day living which becomes distorted in the process of hypnosis.

Leader and subordinate

In every social group a leader naturally arises. Lesser leaders accept this authority and direct still others, thus establishing a "pecking order" or chain of command. Yet each member of a group generally determines his or her own course.

The Bible supports this principle condemning insubordination and implying that leaders are ordained by God. (See Romans 13:1 and Matthew 22:21).

Leadership and authority depend on society. Even animal societies operate by this principle. Hypnotic submission resembles voluntary submission to leadership, except that it distorts the normal relationship between supervisor and subordinate.

Let's consider some basic ideas about suggestibility to see how this relationship is affected by hypnosis.

Suggestion and suggestibility

Suggestion, or the offering of ideas, is the fundamental method of teaching. It aids experience in the process of learning. "Therapeutic suggestion" attempts to improve troublesome thought patterns or to revise distorted viewpoints. Hypnosis, although not necessarily a tool in therapeutic suggestion, is sometimes used in an attempt to eliminate resistance and achieve uncritical acceptance.

Suggestibility is the normal capacity to accept or respond to suggestion. It varies in intensity from indifference to unquestioning obedience. The greater the suggestibility, the less discrimination and deliberation occur in accepting suggestion. Important in this discussion is the boundary where normal suggestibility blends into the hyper-suggestibility of hypnosis. Normally a person retains and exercises discrimination and self-control, but in hypnotism, this important capacity is surrendered.

Normal response to suggestion

Throughout nature individuals tend to follow those who demonstrate initiative and communicate suggestion. Group response to suggestion is seen in "herd instinct." For instance, sheep tend to follow a leader; and a herd of cattle stare at a stranger until one of them runs. Then, acting on that suggestion, the entire group runs in the same direction. A slight disturbance sends a school of fish streaking through the water, not in random confusion but in a protective pattern. In most societies, when two people meet and one extends his hand, the other tends to complete the handshake. Thus suggestibility makes an orderly society possible.

Conversion and the limits of normal suggestion

In evangelism the Holy Spirit influences individuals and brings conviction to their hearts. His human agents cooperate by the sanctified use of suggestion. Thus, through music, prayers, and exhortation, God's Spirit prepares the audience for the altar call. When an appeal is made, listeners are led to crystallize and confirm a decision which previous study has implanted. The public declaration of surrender to Christ strengthens the will and helps the worshiper remain loyal.

On the other hand, abuse may occur in the name of evangelism. Individuals or groups may be hypnotized in a public meeting. Some believe that Adolph Hitler dominated the German people by mass hypnotism. Rock concerts wield a similar captivating power.

The process of conversion is discussed at length by William Sargant in his book, *Battle for the Mind*.[1] In his foreword, he suggests that conversion, whether religious, political, or intellectual, involves alteration of basic attitudes, beliefs and concepts. This change in loyalty may be based on logical study and discovery, or it may come through suggestion when the brain function is severely disturbed. The intense stress associated with the disturbed brain function seems to produce a stirring up or "liquification" of the underlying background of accepted information against which incoming ideas are weighed. Suggestions made while the mind is in such a state of flux may influence this background reference area to resettle into new patterns of accepted basic "truth." Thereafter, incoming ideas are measured by these revised standards.

So-called brainwashing exceeds the normal use of suggestion. Under such severe stress, many are induced to endorse values which they had previously opposed. Without resorting to stress, hypnotherapists often hope to achieve a similar result by implanting suggestions while discrimination and cautious resistance are reduced or eliminated by hypnosis.

Reference

1. William Sargant, *Battle for the Mind: A Physiology of Conversion and Brain-washing*, Doubleday Company, New York, 1957.

Hypnosis

We have seen that a wonderful mechanism efficiently focuses our awareness on a small segment of the innumerable signals constantly seeking attention. Thus, the vast majority of incoming signals are ignored. Furthermore, priority is assigned to those being considered. We have seen that focusing and sorting are influenced by suggestion, and that the normal mental quality of suggestibility may be misused.

Discrimination, the other concept important in our discussion, you probably already understand. It is used in valuing and in the recognition of right and wrong. With an understanding of awareness, suggestibility, and discrimination, we are ready to discuss hypnosis.

Definition

The hypnotic trance is a package-like phenomenon [1] which includes: (1) an increased degree of suggestibility, (2) an alteration or distortion of awareness, and (3) a reduction or loss of the power to discriminate. An individual's capacities of suggestibility, awareness and discrimination naturally vary. However, *when these factors are controlled by another individual, we call the process hypnosis.* In this state a person's will — the ability to decide and act independently — is relinquished, and the will of the hypnotist is accepted in its place. The awareness thus becomes subject to alteration by the hypnotist's suggestion.

Characteristics of hypnosis

1. Not everyone can be hypnotized.

2. It is difficult, if not impossible, to hypnotize a person against his or her will.

3. Babies cannot be hypnotized, but children are more susceptible than older people.

4. People may be hypnotized as individuals or as members of a group.

5. To enter the hypnotic trance, a person must desire hypnosis and believe that it will occur. Trust and confidence, which amounts to faith in the hypnotist, must replace fear.

6. Susceptibility may be increased by an urge to please the hypnotist, by repetition and by fatigue.

7. As the trance deepens, response becomes more absolute.

8. Hypnotic influence may continue after release from the trance.

9. The hypnotized individual risks being used as an instrument by an unscrupulous hypnotist.

Now to expand some of these points: Susceptibility to trance may increase with repetition. This perhaps occurs through learning mechanisms.[2] Bernheim,[3] who practiced hypnosis extensively, made this observation: "Many persons . . . are influenced at the very first seance, others not until the second or third. After being hypnotized once or twice, they are speedily influenced. . . . Patients in whom hypnotic suggestibility is very well developed [respond], however slight may be the idea of sleep that is given them."

Those who recognize the moral accountability for self-control, which accompanies the freedom of God's grace, will appreciate Ellen White's warning: "No individual should be permitted to take control of another person's mind . . . . Temporary relief may be felt, but the mind of the one thus controlled is never again so strong and reliable."[4]

As rapport on a one-to-one basis increases between a willing individual and a hypnotist, the depth and certainty of response increase.

Hypnosis requires trust. To produce confidence during the induction of a trance, the hypnotist often predicts that his subject will experience certain sensations which would be felt anyway but might remain unnoticed. The hypnotist suggests a few little maneuvers to divert attention. As the subject complies with these suggestions and discovers that the predicted sensations are occurring, confidence develops. He tells himself, "Sure enough I am being hypnotized." Releasing his self-determination, the trance begins.

Hypnotists often assure their prospective subjects that hypnotized persons cannot be caused to do anything contrary to their basic standards of right and wrong. Unfortunately, however, most of us seem to have inherited tendencies toward evil. Some authorities on the subject assert that one who has a repressed inner urge to commit some criminal act might readily do so when the restraining effect of better judgment has been removed and the act is suggested by the hypnotist.[5, 6]

Bernard C. Gindes, discussing hypnosis as an adjunct to psychotherapy, says, " . . . I have expressed the opinion that with adequate conditioning criminal acts can be facilitated through hypnosis. . . . I would not underestimate the potential capacity of a strong suggestion in an adaptable mind."[6]

Furthermore, mind control does not necessarily end when the hypnosis session is over. By "therapeutic suggestion" psychoanalysts believe hypnosis enables them to implant impressions in the subconscious minds of their patients. For instance, "Even though you relinquish all active control over a subject when you awaken him, the posthypnotic suggestions you have made still control him and his thoughts and actions. They have become . . . an integral part of his mental process. . . .

"The continued control of the hypnotist over the subject's subjective mind leads to a gradually increasing influence over the subject's objective process as well, and thus to a remodeling of his entire thought pattern. This is the basis of therapeutic hypnosis based upon implantation of suggestions in the subject's subjective mind with continuing (posthypnotic) effects."[7]

How hypnosis is induced

Hypnosis is not entertainment! I urge you to avoid all involvement with its practice. Don't even watch it.

The importance of understanding how a person is guided into hypnotic trance will become evident when we look at possession and some of Satan's religious counterfeits in the next chapter.

Bernard C. Gindes[8] defines for the would-be hypnotist "the hypnotic formula." Particularly notice two points: first, how confidence in the hypnotist resembles what the Christian calls faith; and second, the necessity of diverting the subject's attention.

"The actual mechanism of hypnosis depends upon a fixed formula; when this is carried out meticulously, hypnosis *must* follow . . . . MISDIRECTED ATTENTION + BELIEF + EXPECTATION = THE HYPNOTIC STATE."

Creating these conditions for the hypnotic state involves diverting the mind from questioning what is happening, personal surrender to the hypnotist, and building up expectation.

"Imagination is the integrating factor which welds belief and expectation into an irresistible force. Fear can be utilized for added stimulus; the subject's wish to depart from 'reality' causes him to welcome hypnosis as a desired experience. The subject's entire personality must be aligned with the aid of imagination in a definite course to aid and abet the experienced hypnotist."[8].

Some of the many variations in behavior which may occur as a result of hypnosis are described in the chapter about my own experience. Other examples are alluded to in discussing spirit possession and glossolalia.   The following section considers conditions which are often confused with hypnosis.

Conditions resembling hypnosis

A number of hypnosis-like (hypnoid) states probably depend on the neurophysiologic mechanism involved in hypnosis.   In typical *hysteria,* a trance-like distortion of awareness, and perhaps behavior, develops in a person under severe emotional stress.   This often seems to serve a useful function in diverting the attention of the person himself and/or others from an intolerable problem. Or it may, for a time, side step making a painful decision or taking other undesired action. Because of this, it is sometimes called a "conversion reaction."

While isolated examples of hysteria are seen related to the stressful variations of everyday life, probably the most dramatic and severe examples of major hysteria are war neuroses.

"Very many of the more spectacular reactions to war stresses could be labeled as 'anxiety hysteria.' Indeed, one of the commonest final reactions to stress in patients of previously stable temperament, as opposed to the unstable, was the development of hysterical responses . . . .

"Once a state of hysteria has been induced . . . by mounting stresses which the brain can no longer tolerate, protective inhibition is likely to supervene. This will disturb the individual's ordinary conditioned behavior patterns. . . . states of greatly increased suggestibility are also found; and so are their opposite, namely, states in which the patient is deaf to all suggestions, however sensible . . . .

"Critical faculties may become inhibited in these states of anxiety hysteria. . . . Police forces in many parts of the world rely on this inhibition of critical faculties and normal judgment to obtain full confessions from prisoners subjected to debilitation or emotional stresses, without the need to injure them physically."[9]

Hysteria and hypnosis resemble each other in several ways

but they differ in one very important respect. Hypnosis requires surrender of the will to another individual. By contrast, in cases of major hysteria, the affected person's ability to cope has been exhausted by the fatigue of prolonged, excessive emotional stress until his mental processes are simply out of order. Of course the Christian may look to God's promise: "Those of steadfast mind you keep in peace—in peace because they trust in you." (Isaiah 26:3).

Autohypnosis (or self-hypnosis) is said to be the cause of behaviors with many features typical of hypnosis except that no hypnotist is recognized. Some consider hysteria to be self-hypnosis. Conversely, hypnosis has been described as artificially induced hysteria. Some also equate glossolalia, spirit possession and spirit medium experiences with self-hypnosis.

But the idea of hypnotizing one's self is illogical. How does one surrender self-control to himself without still being in control? Generally, cases called self-hypnosis may be explained as post-hypnotic influence, as hysteria, or as possession by a supernatural spirit. And in the final analysis, are we not looking at the same basic phenomena in different packages? Is not the same satanic power the real agency in control—perhaps even in hysteria? We must ask similar questions about the supernatural influences in Eastern religions. An element of transcendental meditation resembles hypnosis. This will be discussed when we comment on possession in the next chapter.

A delusion of the last days

In their book, *The Seduction of Christianity,* Hunt and McMahon recognize hypnotism as part of the world influence often called the New Age Movement.[10]

"It requires little insight to realize that in order to establish Antichrist's official world religion in the space age, where science is worshiped, it will be necessary to merge religion with science. . . .

"One place where science and religion have met is in the growing practice of hypnosis. Though an integral part of occultism for thousands of years, hypnosis has now been accepted as 'scientific' and is even being used by hundreds of Christian psychologists."[10]

References

1. Louis J. West, "Psychophysiology of Hypnosis," *The Journal of the American Medical Association,* Feb. 13, 1960, Vol. 172, p. 672. Copyright 1960, American Medical Association.

2. Andre M. Weitzenhoefer, *General Technique of Hypnotism,* p. 271. Grune & Stratton. New York, 1957.

3. H. Bernheim, (Trans. from 2nd rev. ed. by Christian Herter), *Hypnosis & Suggestion in Psychotherapy,* p. 4. University Books. New Hyde Park, New York, 1964.

4. Ellen G. White, *Medical Ministry,* pp. 115, 116. Pacific Press. Nampa, Idaho, 1963.

5. Bernard Hollander, *Methods and Uses of Hypnosis & Self-hypnosis,* Page 170 in the 1979 edition published by Melvin Powers, Wilshire Book Company, North Hollywood, California. First published in London, 1935.

6. Bernard C. Gindes, *New Concepts of Hypnosis,* p. 93. Copyright 1951 by Bernard C. Gindes, M.D. Renewed © 1979 by Hanna E. Gindes. Used by permission of The Julian Press, Inc. Also see: Louis J. West and Gordon H. Deckert, *Journal of the American Medical Association,* April 5, 1956, Vol. 192, pp. 9-12. Copyright 1965, American Medical Association.

7. Raphael H. Rhodes, *Hypnosis,* pp. 116, 117. The Citadel Press. Secaucus, New Jersey, 1950.

8. Bernard C. Gindes, *Op. Cit.,* pp. 77, 78.

9. William Sargant, *Battle for the Mind: A Physiology of Conversion and Brain-washing,* pp. 59, 60. Doubleday & Company. Garden City, New York, 1957.

10. Dave Hunt and T. A. McMahon, *The Seduction of Christianity,* p. 73. Harvest House Publishers, Eugene, OR 97402, 1985. Also see: William Kroger and William Fezler, *Hypnosis and Behavior Modification: Imagery Conditioning,* p. 412. J. B. Lippincott Co., Philadelphia, PA 19105. 1976. And: Kenneth R. Wade (not related to the author), *Secrets of the New Age,* Review and Herald Pub. Assn., Hagerstown, MD, 1989.

Possession

Now we turn from hypnosis to consider the interesting New Testament phenomenon we call *possession*. After exploring the concept of possession, we will examine its relationship to various forms of good and evil mind control.

What we mean by possession

My dictionary suggests that to possess is to have, to own, to control, to occupy, to dominate, and to strongly influence. All of these characteristics pertain to the special variety of possession we are considering. Specifically, we are talking about the influence of a supernatural being in the lives and actions of people.

First, we believe that supernatural spirits exist and are able to communicate with mankind. We also assume that the awareness capacity has several overlapping components. The first is intellect. We reason with this component. It deals with words, numbers, ideas and theories. Second is the emotional component, sometimes called the heart. Here we deal with intuitive feelings and subconscious impressions. The third component we define as spiritual. This spiritual nature is distinct in many ways although some may wish to include it as a subdivision of emotional awareness.

Before we can relate and coordinate these variations of awareness to possession, we need to define communication.

Communication

Communication is the transfer of thoughts and feelings from one individual to another. Communication requires both giving and receiving. In other words, speaking is not communication unless someone is listening and comprehending. Communication is essentially of three kinds: verbal, nonverbal, and spiritual.

Communication from intellect to intellect is chiefly verbal. Lecturing, preaching, writing, and printing are typical modes of verbal communication.

Nonverbal communication is largely heart-to-heart. It is conveyed by attitude, gestures and manner. If the verbal message contradicts the nonverbal message, the latter is the one usually perceived.

Spiritual communication is a third type. A supernatural spirit may communicate directly with the mind of a person without using the ordinary sensory mechanisms. This may comprise impressions or a distinct message.

Considering the perfection of the original creation,d over the following assumption seems valid: We know that God is a spirit (John 4:24). Surely the infinitely wise and loving Creator provided a mechanism whereby His Spirit could communicate directly with creatures made in His own image. This assumption is compatible with the following statement of Ellen White. "The brain nerves that connect with the whole system are the medium through which heaven communicates with man, and affects the inmost life."[1] In other words, we assume that there was, and is, a mechanism whereby the Holy Spirit can communicate directly with each of us.

Zechariah describes a golden bowl with pipes leading to seven lamps. He saw olive branches filling the bowl (Zech. 4:1-13). In commenting on this, Ellen White suggests that God has an organized, effective channel of communication. "Through the golden pipes, the olive branches empty the oil out of themselves. These olive branches are the anointed ones that stand by the Lord of the whole earth. Through them the Holy Spirit is communicated to the churches. . . . The power that is in heaven unites with human intelligences."[2] "By the holy beings surrounding His throne, the Lord keeps up a constant communication with the inhabitants of the earth. The golden oil represents the grace with which God keeps the lamps of believers supplied."[3]

Some persons exploring occult phenomena and parapsychology consider extrasensory perception (or ESP) to be an undeveloped, latent sense. Experiments with extrasensory perception, if they are not delusional, may be dealing with this very mechanism which we have been discussing.

Possession, a mystery

Do not be dismayed if we touch on ideas which are not easily grasped. We have been discussing problems which have been studied by many scholars. All admit that the mechanism within the brain which produces awareness, thought, decision making, and logical action is not really understood. Thus, in contemplating spirit possession, we project our thinking only a little further into the unknown.

Possession by the Holy Spirit

Possession by the Holy Spirit is a Biblical concept. Notice, for example, Romans 8:9: "But you are not in the flesh; you are in the Spirit, since the Spirit of God dwells in you." And 1 Corinthians 3: 16: "Do you not know that you are God's temple and that God's spirit dwells in you?"

Ellen White has written, "When the soul surrenders itself to Christ, a new power takes possession of the new heart. A change is wrought which man can never accomplish for himself. It is a supernatural work, bringing a supernatural element into human nature. The soul that is yielded to Christ, becomes His own fortress, which He holds in a revolted world, and He intends that no authority shall be known in it but His own. A soul thus kept in possession by the heavenly agencies, is impregnable to the assaults of Satan. But unless we do yield ourselves to the control of Christ, we shall be dominated by the wicked one. We must inevitably be under the control of the one or the other of the two great powers that are contending for the supremacy of the world."[4]

Surrender to Christ clearly involves a free choice. Actually, we are not defeated by Christ, as though He overpowers us. Instead it is more like enlisting in His army. We do not enter a state of passive hyper-suggestibility. Our Creator chooses to be served only by truly free creatures. Hence a person fully surrendered to God's control, acts and lives in harmony with the divine will because he has chosen that will as his own. I believe it was God's original plan that the influence of the Holy Spirit should be complete and unchallenged.

Possession by an unholy spirit

Now we turn to the other side of the path where we will examine an entirely different kind of possession — possession by an unholy spirit. Such possession results from submission to the suggestions of an evil spirit. It seems reasonable to believe that the mechanism designed for communication with the Holy Spirit may be usurped by agents of the evil one. In comparing these two kinds of possession we expect to find a difference determined by the contrast in the characters of the possessors.

Unclean spirits mentioned in Scripture

In the Scriptural account of one case which some of us might have diagnosed as epilepsy, a father asking Jesus for help, described his possessed son's condition in these words: "Suddenly a spirit seizes him, and all at once he shrieks. It convulses him until he foams at the mouth; it mauls him and will scarcely leave him" (Luke 9:39).

In other cases, individuals seem to have been dominated by supernatural spirits in the sense of possession as described in this study. For example, Acts 8:7 reports that "unclean spirits, crying with loud shrieks, came out of many who were possessed."

In his book, *The Mind Possessed,* British psychiatrist, William Sargant, helps clarify the phenomenon of possession.[5]

In England, he experienced the violent World War II bombing raids. After the war he spent time in Africa, Haiti and Tennessee making friends with witch doctors, voodoo priests, and faith healers. He watched them at work and observed the altered awareness which occurred in their subjects. In this book, he compares these phenomena with those observed in persons experiencing hypnotic trance. He discusses "Beatles possession" which occurs during rock music festivals. He describes how hypersuggestibility makes ideas and behavior contagious in groups. He comments on the weakening of individual will power under the influence of a popular dynamic leader. And he mentions how a strong desire to please a hypnotist produces "blind obedience" to even absurd commands and to posthypnotic suggestion.

Methods facilitating the development of Beatle trance-like ecstasy are very similar to those which lead to spirit control at voodoo dances, and also resemble factors which induce group hypnosis. Namely, attention is diverted and then compromised by fatigue. Fatigue is produced by the physical exertion of frantic dancing and is accentuated by loud, pounding, somewhat dysrhythmic, music. Eager anticipation and high expectation that ecstasy will occur also contribute significantly. In the case of the rock concert, a strong desire to please the greatly-admired rock star is an important factor. Whether the star serves as hypnotist, or whether he participates with the audience in mass spirit possession may be debatable. Interestingly, Sargant found voodoo, where control by a supernatural spirit is deliberately sought, similar to Beatle possession. In rock music, as in the music of voodoo and devil dancing, melody is eclipsed by enchanting rhythm. It cannot be sanctified by association with words of the Christian religion.

Spiritism

Spiritism (or spiritualism) is one type of possession. Notice Paul's caution in 1 Timothy 4:1: "Now the [Holy] Spirit expressly says that in latter times some will renounce the faith by paying attention to deceitful spirits and teachings of demons."

Spiritism has been with us since the serpent induced the woman to take the forbidden fruit. He told her, "You will not die; for God knows that when you eat of it your eyes will be opened, and you will be like God, knowing good and evil" (Gen. 3:4).

The message of spiritism to mankind has not changed. It teaches that death is merely a step into a more favorable existence. Leroy Froom in his book, *Spiritualism Today*,[6] quotes extensively from spiritualist and other authors. He crystallizes the position of spiritism very well: "The 'spirits' of spiritualism, and their exponents, attack the very foundations of Christianity itself by denying the inspiration and authority of Holy Scripture, denying the deity of Jesus Christ as the second person of the Godhead, denying the reality and sovereignty of His judgment . . . and His power to resurrect all men at the last day, denying the actuality of sin and the need for and reality of redemption, and denying the ultimate destruction of all unrepentant sinners. That disavowal is decisive."

Leslie M. LeCron and Jean Bordeaux make the following comments concerning spiritualism, "When in a trance . . . the medium seems to come under the control of another personality, purportedly the spirit of a departed soul, and a genuine medium undoubtedly believes the 'control' to be a spiritual entity.

"In the trance, the medium often enters a cataleptic state marked by extreme rigidity. The control then takes over, the voice may change completely . . . and the supposed spirit answers the questions of the sitter, telling of things 'on the other plane' and giving messages from those who have 'passed over.'"[7]

"LeCron . . . was able to discuss this relationship with . . . Stewart White, famous writer whose latest works were devoted to spiritualism. Sincere and completely convinced as to the validity of spiritualism after a quarter century of intensive study of the subject, White volunteered to try to obtain information on hypnosis from his control, whom he termed 'the Gaelic.' In a subsequent seance this entity from the 'Unobstructed Universe,' which White believed controlled him during a trance, undertook an explanation which was a new interpretation and one of great interest. It was stated by him that hypnosis and the mediumistic trance are definitely identical but that they should not be considered autohypnosis. The medium having made himself relaxed and receptive, the invisibles (as White termed them) from their plane induce the hypnotic state! And they often find it as difficult as does a corporeal hypnotist, according to the Gaelic control."[8]

After reporting this interview, Dr. LeCron comments that many spiritualistic messages are "assigned to spirit origin, the information thereby disclosed assertedly being unknown to the conscious mind . . . ."[9] From my point of view, however, the mediumistic trance is a phenomenon which we call possession. The trance is induced by a supernatural spirit acting as hypnotist.

Ellen White makes the following interesting comment: "There are few who have any just conception of the deceptive power of spiritualism and the danger of coming under its influence. Many tamper with it merely to gratify their curiosity. They have no real faith in it and would be filled with horror at the thought of yielding themselves to the spirits' control. But they venture upon the forbidden ground, and the mighty destroyer exercises his power upon them against their will. Let them once be induced to submit their minds to his direction, and he holds them captive. It is impossible, in their own strength, to break away from the bewitching, alluring spell."[10] This suggests that a state resembling posthypnotic influence may persist after such an experience.

One further word is in order concerning the nature of supernatural spirits. The Bible does not support the idea of the transmigration of the soul. Angels were created as angels from the beginning. They are supernatural beings. Humans were created as humans and will always be such.

In John 11:11-14, Jesus calls the first death "sleep." Ecclesiastes 9:5, 6 and John 5:28, 29 make it clear that this sleep state continues until it is terminated by the resurrection, when "all who are in the tombs will hear his voice, and will come out. . . ." Thus there are no "departed" human spirits to practice possession or to communicate with anyone. (See Job 7:12 and 14:21). However, the Scriptures do declare the existence of evil angels (Rev. 12:7-9; Jude 6) or evil spirits (Luke 8:2).

Transcendental meditation

The meditation practiced by adherents of several Eastern religions involves a type of trance which appears to be a form of spirit possession. As an example, many Hindus believe that transcendental meditation blends the devotee's spirit with the higher all-pervading universal spirit. This state is sought while sitting motionless in the "lotus" position after ritual bodily purification. The devout Hindu makes an effort to subdue and eliminate all physical and voluntary mental activity in submission to the divine spirit so that the blissful state of nirvana may be achieved.

A little book entitled *The Daily Practice of the Hindus,*[11] provides insights into the practice of the Hindu faith. It contains several devotional chants, called "mantras," and tells how they are used.

For example, as soon as the believer awakens in the morning he is to recite, "Let Brahma, Vishnu, the foe of Mura, Shiva, the slayer of Tripura, the Sun, Moon, Mars, Mercury, Jupiter, Venus, Saturn, the ascending and the descending Nodes, let all (the Celestials) make the morning auspicious for me."

After reciting certain mantras, or formal prayers, the believer is to make a mental program of his day's work, then he rises from the bed, touches the earth with his right foot and repeats, "O Earth, the giver of all that is good to us, I bow before Thee."

One of the purification mantras states, "Om! Raising the Jiva-monad from the Muladhara (lit. Elemental-Mountain), slowly through the Susumna channel of the spinal cord, I unite it with the Supreme Monad in the head. Svaba."

Thus transcendental meditation as described in these practices invites spirit control. Similar spirit connections are fundamental components of other Eastern religions such as Buddhism and Brahmanism. And all obviously counterfeit God's original plan for divine guidance.

Double occupancy

Before considering the relationship between possession and hypnosis, we should ask whether the Holy Spirit and an evil spirit can dwell in a person simultaneously. Jesus said, "No one can serve two masters; for a slave will either hate the one and love the other, or be devoted to the one and despise the other" (Matt. 6:24). Even more significantly, God has declared, "You shall have no other gods before me" (Ex. 20:3). Presuming to divide our loyalty between two lords just doesn't work.

In Matthew 12:43-45, our Saviour tells about a man who had been released from domination by an unclean spirit. It says his house was clean. Apparently he determined to live strictly on his own, without allowing the Holy Spirit to have possession of his soul temple. But in the end he was in a far worse condition than before he was cleansed. In other words, the soul temple is designed and built for spiritual occupancy. It is not enough that one be freed from the domination of Satan. If life is to be ultimately successful, one must be willing to accept the influence of the Holy Spirit.

Possession and hypnosis

The trance-like state of spirit possession is remarkably similar in appearance and mannerism to the hypnotic trance. Because of this similarity, and because no hypnotist is seen to be responsible, most observers assume that spirit possession is simply self-hypnosis. But, how can one hypnotize himself? If I surrender control of my mind to myself, am I not still in control? This appears to be a contradiction of terms, unless we view all hypnosis as evil spirit possession.

It is my personal conviction that the normal human brain is capable of experiencing the functional relation to the Holy Spirit by a mechanism which is misused to achieve hypnotic trance. Furthermore, I believe this capacity of the mind of man was designed to permit communion with the Holy Spirit. God uses it when He gives dreams and visions to His prophets. He uses it in a milder, non-trance-like manner in providing normal spiritual guidance to His children through the conscience. This mechanism may be surrendered to the control of an evil spirit as occurs in voodoo spirit possession; or a human hypnotist may intrude into the relationship when he casts a spell over his subject.

Stated differently, spiritual possession implies responding to the suggestions of a supernatural spirit. As every salesman knows, an increase in responsiveness naturally occurs as one accepts suggestions. Therefore, as would be expected, responding repeatedly to the suggestions of a supernatural spirit, including the Holy Spirit, tends to make one more susceptible to the influence of that spirit. Such increased susceptibility also occurs as rapport increases between a hypnotist and his subject. In hypnotic trance, the depth of response to suggestion may vary from slight to profound. The intensity of response to spirit possession may vary in a similar way.

The quiet, unobtrusive influence of the Holy Spirit in the life of a Christian seems to be imitated by the post hypnotic influence which some hypnotherapists hope will benefit their patients. In both cases an internal guiding force is at work without evidence of a trance.

Glossolalia

The ecstasy experienced while speaking in an "unknown tongue" resembles the trance of spirit possession and that of hypnosis. For this reason, glossolalia deserves careful examination.

At the outset, we may accept the obvious truth that any behavior is unsafe if it disregards basic principles clearly taught in the Scriptures. God does not contradict Himself. No matter how impressive such manifestations may be, they cannot replace Scripture study as a basis for belief and practice.

Personally, I know a number of people who speak in tongues. I admire them. They are conscientious and sincere. Yet, I must explain my misgivings concerning the nature of this "gift" as it is commonly practiced. Remember that when the disciples were all filled with the Holy Spirit at Pentecost, they "began to speak with other languages, as the Spirit gave them ability. Now there were devout Jews from every nation under heaven living in Jerusalem. . . . each one heard them speaking in the native language of each" (Acts 2:4-6).

In this case they spoke in *other* tongues, suggesting that they communicated in a language with which they were unfamiliar. But miraculously, they were understood by all who heard. Effective purpose was obvious in this experience.

In harmony with our earlier discussion, we may assume that the Holy Spirit, or a divine messenger, or an evil angel may communicate with a human being through direct mental suggestion, just as the human hypnotist evidently influences his subject by verbal suggestion.

Those who speak in an "unknown tongue" believe that their voice is controlled by the Holy Spirit, and that they are not personally responsible for the sounds produced. Their utterances are considered to be "the language of heaven" and hence not necessarily intelligible to people. They seem to be in a sort of trance, unaware of what is happening around them. Some feel that, during this process, their will is replaced by the Holy Spirit's total control. But God's Spirit does not work that way. The chapter, "Will and Salvation," reveals that, in submitting to God, the will is harmonized with His will while the individual remains in control.

We may reasonably question whether exercise of the "tongues" experience is evidence of being possessed by the Spirit of God. We are told that Satan appears as an "angel of light" (2 Cor. 11:14). Counterfeit money does not deceive anyone unless it closely resembles genuine money. This applies as well to counterfeit speaking in tongues.

Glossolalia at Corinth

The gift of tongues was important in the early church. Paul devoted about one fifth of his first letter to the church at Corinth (Chapters 12, 13, 14) to this problem. He gently but clearly put the issue in perspective. Probably he was writing to people who earnestly believed that ecstatic, seemingly unintelligible, speech was of divine origin. Paul did not condemn the Corinthian brethren. He carefully avoided driving away any sincere worshiper. "Now, brothers and sisters," he writes, "if I come to you speaking in tongues, how will I benefit you unless I bring you some revelation or knowledge or prophecy or teaching?" (1 Cor. 14:6). "I thank

God that I speak in tongues more than all of you; nevertheless, in church I would rather speak five words with my mind, in order to instruct others also, than ten thousand words in a tongue" (1 Cor. 14:18, 19).

In other words, Paul seems to be saying, "If I come to you speaking a language you do not understand, how shall I benefit you?" By "speaking in tongues more than all of you," he probably referred to his ability to speak Aramaic, Hebrew, Greek, and maybe other languages.

Furthermore, in chapter 13, Paul emphasizes that even the genuine gift of tongues is of little significance compared to the greater gifts of faith, hope and love. By implication, he seems to be saying that unintelligible ecstatic speech, which could not convince or persuade unbelievers, was not to be desired.

Glossolalia is a miraculous experience, but miracles are not necessarily evidence that God's power is at work. We are told about deceptive miracles. (Rev. 13:14. See also 2 Thess. 2:8-10 and Rev. 16:14).

Evaluation of the trance often associated with the popular speaking in tongues deserves caution. We should be willing to be used but should never attempt to use the Holy Spirit or to command Him to do our bidding.

Possession summarized
William Sargant[12] observes that the same psychological processes are involved in spirit possession, the gift of tongues, utterances of mediums, faith healing, some aspects of the witch doctor's activity, and behavior under hypnosis.

Ellen White, possession and hypnosis
The following remarks illustrate Ellen White's attitude toward possession:

"Every man is free to choose what power he will have to rule over him."[13] "God does not control our minds without our consent; but if we desire to know and to do His will these promises are ours: 'If any man willeth to do His will, he shall know of the teaching.'"[14]

"Those who turn from the plain teaching of Scripture and the convicting power of the Holy Spirit are inviting the control of demons. . . . Agencies are at work which are but the medium of lying spirits. Many a man tampers with these merely from curiosity, but . . . he is lured on and on, until he is controlled by a will stronger than his own. He cannot escape from its mysterious power."[15]

As you are probably aware, Ellen White opposes the use of hypnosis. For example she says, "The theory of mind controlling mind was originated by Satan. . . . It opens a door through which Satan will enter to take possession both of the mind that is given up to be controlled . . . and of the mind that controls."[16]

Ellen White's attitude is not one of personal aversion. It is not a superstitious taboo. By examining the problem, we can discover a basic moral principle which shows that her warnings are not groundless. We have noticed the essential nature of hypnosis. We observed that, although suggestibility is God-given, hypersuggestibility is abnormal whether induced by hypnosis or due to stress as in hysteria. In hysteria, the will may be crushed, but it is not surrendered to another individual as in hypnosis.

Self-control, and the capacity to discriminate, to evaluate and to choose a course of action are vitally important. Whether these abilities are retained or surrendered is a spiritual and moral issue. Its significance will be considered in subsequent chapters.

Very early in Ellen White's ministry, certain people suggested that her visions were the result of being hypnotized.[17] People around her knew that she was not acting like her usual self, and they could not see or hear what she was experiencing. Actually there is good reason to affirm that the visions of Ellen White were not produced by hypnosis, but that her mind was possessed by the Holy Spirit during those experiences.[18]

For example, many concepts of proper diet and hygiene which Ellen White endorsed and promoted were championed by relatively few people one hundred years ago. And those who did accept the ideas were often considered faddists and quacks. However, during the past few decades dramatic changes have occurred in the thinking of a majority of serious students of nutrition. This near reversal of attitude is an example of the evidence that deepens my belief that her work was directly influenced by the Holy Spirit.

We must return to the problem of hypnotism. Why did Ellen White oppose hypnotism? Is it morally wrong? Does it matter whether one's will and discrimination are surrendered to someone else?

References

1. Ellen G. White, *Education,* Pacific Press. Nampa, Idaho, 1903.

2. _____ *Review and Herald,* May 16, 1899.

3. _____ *Seventh-day Adventist Bible Commentary,* vol. 4, p. 1179, Review and Herald. Hagerstown, Maryland, 1957.

4. _____ *The Desire of Ages,* Pacific Press, 1940. p. 324.

5. William Sargant, *The Mind Possessed: A Physiology of Possession, Mysticism, and Faith Healing,* Harper & Row, New York, 1974. The Beatles were the first popular rock music group.

6. Leroy Froom, *Spiritualism Today,* p. 33. Review and Herald, 1963

7. Leslie M. LeCron and Jean Bordeaux, *Hypnotism Today,* p. 154. Grun and Stratton, New York, 1947.

8. *Ibid,* p. 156.

9. *Ibid,* p. 157.

10. Ellen G. White, *The Great Controversy,* Pacific Press, 1911.

11. Srisa Chandra Vasu, *The Daily Practice of the Hindus, Containing the Morning and Midday Duties,* 2nd Edition, Allahabad, India, Undated.

12. William Sargant, *Op. Cit.,* p. 194.

13. Ellen G. White, *The Desire of Ages,* p. 258.

14. *Ibid,* p. 258.

15. *Ibid,* p. 258.

16. Ellen G. White, *The Ministry of Healing,* p. 243. Pacific Press, 1909.

17. Ellen G. White, *Early Writings,* p. 21. Review and Herald, 1945.

18. *Ibid,* pp. 39, 40.

Evil spirit control

Do not fear, for I am with you,
do not be afraid, for I am your God;
I will strengthen you, I will help you,
I will uphold you with my victorious right hand.
Yes, all who are incensed against you
shall be ashamed and disgraced;
those who strive against you
shall be as nothing
and shall perish (Isaiah 41:10, 11).

A matter of choice

In this chapter, I'm going to tell you about a young lady who had a frightful experience with evil spirit possession. My purpose is not entertainment. And it's not to inform you that such things happen; tragically, stories like this are all too common. I want you to see, in this account and in the ones Pastor Gessele relates in the next chapter, first, how satanic control or release from it depends on the choice of the individual; and second, how, through our prayer relationship with God, His Spirit can release those who choose His freedom. (Names have been changed, but the stories are true.)

In each instance the mental function of the affected individual is obviously abnormal. However, opinions differ concerning the conditions and causes producing these types of strange behavior. The educational background which shapes the understanding of the different observers tints or glaringly colors their conclusions.

I believe that the sincere Christian should develop a

philosophical stance which sees scientific observation as a legitimate source of truth within the bounds our Creator has opened for our study. Without such a harmonizing position, the conclusions of persons trained to understand the working of the human mind will remain incompatible with the views of those who have studied mostly in the domain of theology.

Sandy's encounter with evil

For several weeks Sandy and her roommate at a Christian boarding school had been secretly listening to rock music records. She was depressed and couldn't concentrate on her studies. She began having headaches and frightful nightmares. The girls were afraid to tell anyone what was really going on.

One afternoon Sandy fainted. When she revived, the dean urged her to lie down and relax. That evening the two girls played one of their records again. Satan seemed to be speaking in the background in a horrifying manner. Sandy began to cry and scream. Someone called her brother at the boy's dormitory.

When he arrived, Sandy seemed to look right through him, eyes glaring with panic. He and the boy's dean tried to restrain her, feeling she might hurt herself. But she easily pushed them aside with her scant 90 pounds. Whenever someone would start to pray, she would scream and laugh with a hideous deep voice. A Bible was placed in her hand but she threw it aside. Someone asked, "Satan, why don't you get out and leave Sandy alone? She belongs to Jesus."

"I know she belongs to God and you," the voice replied, "but I am going to take all I can get."

Someone in the group found the record and broke it. It was then that God answered their prayers for release. Sandy later explained that she could hear the people around her but that all she could see was the devil sitting beside her on her bed. When the record was broken, she felt release from the power which had controlled her. Then she joined the others in singing and prayer. She clasped her Bible and promised, "I will never let you go again."

The experience made a serious impression on the students, Several of them destroyed rock records and books on magic which they had kept hidden from the deans.

Following this crisis, Sandy was considerably shaken. Gradually her composure and self-confidence returned, and after a few weeks, she seemed to be her usual, happy self.

As this book goes to press, twelve years have passed since the horrible night of Sandy's experience with the evil one. She is now a pastor's wife and a mother. Demon possession or other emotional problems have not recurred.

The greater power

By Pastor Glen Gessele

A few days after Sandy's victory which Dr. Wade related in the previous chapter, I received a call from the boy's dormitory. The student monitor spoke with anxiety. "We need you right away. Bob is possessed!"

Commitment to Satan

I hurried to the dormitory. Bob was threatening harm to himself and to others. The voice of the demon who spoke through him was obviously different from Bob's own voice. Fearing we might be struck, we prayed for the young man with our eyes open. Each time we mentioned the name, "Jesus," the demon would cringe and then after a moment would laugh hideously. The voice would utter statements such as, "There is no Jesus, There is no blood, There is no cross," as if to deny the validity of our prayers.

Because I believe it is unwise to converse with the "father of lies," I asked God to bring victory. I would pray, "Father, although Bob is not in control of his mind just now, we ask that through the blood of Jesus, you would release him from the demons and give him the power to make up his own mind."

Then the demon would leave. The young man, physically exhausted, would relax and talk in his own voice. When we felt that victory had been gained, there would be a resurgence. This occurred two or three times. The demons did not give up easily.

Then Bob jumped out the second story window onto a

roof. The dean and I hurried outside to talk to him. Bob was standing at the edge of the roof with the demon saying, "I'm going to throw Bob down and kill him." Again, without taking my eyes off him, I prayed, "Dear Jesus, we ask that you give Bob control of his own mind and another opportunity to choose what he wants to do with his life." Finally, with much ugliness, the demon said, "All right, all right, I'll leave. But I'll be back again tomorrow night."

The young man was himself again except that he seemed slightly confused and didn't seem to know how he got on the porch roof. I suggested, "Bob, why don't you just turn and lower yourself over the edge. I will be here to help you down." We went back inside, thanking the Lord for the deliverance. As we talked, I asked, "Bob, have you in any way made a commitment to Satan?" He replied, "Yes, I have." We encouraged him to ask God for forgiveness and to claim the greater power that is ours through Jesus. While we were talking, no genuine desire to be Christ's child was apparent, although he was very much afraid of the devil.

The demon did return the following week.

If permitted, Satan is able to slip in and take over a person's mind and body. In Sandy's case, she persistently listened to records which she knew to be forbidden and satanic. Bob was aware that he had made a commitment to serve Satan. Perhaps now his mind had become deformed and was unable to respond to the Holy Spirit. Although shaken by the experience, he did not seem open to our suggestion that he tell the Lord, "I'm sorry. Help me. I'll try again."

Since these cases were common knowledge in the dormitories, all the students were greatly concerned. They read their Bibles and prayed as they had never prayed before. Two other young ladies developed symptoms suggesting lost contact with reality. Whether these were merely fear responses or mild forms of possession was never clear.

Enchanting symbols and music

I think of another experience I had while pastor at the secondary school where Sandy and Bob were students. I was approached by a young man who had been a student there a few years earlier, and who was no longer a practicing Christian. He was married and living in the community. He revealed that he was concerned about the students but even more concerned about himself. He said, "Since I have been exploring witchcraft and the occult, I have been having strange and scary experiences. I see an ugly face hovering over my bed at night." Then before I could respond he added, "But don't pray for me. Just tell me what to do if I should choose to be free from this."

He was afraid that if I prayed, a tremendous struggle would take place and he wasn't ready to make a decision or to endure the struggle. I agreed, "All right. I will not pray in your presence, but when you are gone I will pray." As we continued to talk, he said, "Pastor, I've been hearing about some of the things going on in the dormitories at the school. Is it true that in one of the rooms or in the basement of the boy's dorm, there is a certain symbol on the ceiling or on the wall? I've heard that there's a demon symbol there and I just wanted to share with you my concern, because I don't think these young people know what they're doing." This young man, only two or three years older than some of the students, and not living a Christian life, was worried about them.

He said, "I'm going to tell you why I'm concerned. I've done a lot of reading and study about witchcraft and demon possession and things like this. There's a lot of power in those symbols. Putting up those symbols is an admission that you would like to have devil powers around. I'm afraid for these students." Then he added, "Some of the records that many of us are listening to these days are inspired by demons."

Records of harsh, loud, enchanting music with violent rhythm had become increasingly popular. The subliminal suggestions that came across, and the lyrics containing songs of praise for the devil were also significant. Then he said, "I have some of those records. Would you be interested in hearing them for yourself?"

"Not particularly," I told him. "I'll take your word for it."

"Well, I didn't think you would want to hear them. But, you know, it's dangerous to listen to such records."

I found it hard to believe that he could be concerned for others when he himself was dabbling in this kind of thing.

Problems unresolved

Since that time, I have seen more cases of demon possession. Late one night, I received a phone call urging me to visit a young couple immediately. Bill, the husband, seemed to have lost his mind. I asked a neighboring pastor to accompany me. When we reached Bill's home, he had a knife in his hand and appeared very much possessed. We heard two contrasting voices. One would make threats such as, "I am going to kill him. I am going to stick it in his heart." We prayed for protection. We asked for the knife and he gave it to us. We asked whether he had been convicted that he should turn over to the Lord a certain area of his life which he was unwilling to surrender. The young man replied, "Yes, it's my friends down in the city. I dread to go there because within hours I fall back into my old habits—cursing, swearing, drinking, feeling contempt for spiritual things. That must be where the devil gets into my life. I haven't surrendered that area to the Lord."

Unfortunately Bill's problems didn't end with our visit. For a while he continued having ups and downs. A few years later, he was killed in a dreadful automobile accident. How many such deaths may be devil-inspired suicides, no one knows.

Unwilling

When I conduct a series of spiritual emphasis meetings with students I encourage them to share with me some of the problems and joys they are experiencing. I recall one young lady whose Christian experience wasn't getting anywhere. She had more than the ordinary adolescent fears. I finally asked, "Have you, either in jest or seriously, made a commitment to Satan? Have you ever said something like, 'Satan you can use me,' or 'you can have me,' or 'I dare you to try'?"

At this she looked sharply at me and asked, "How did you know?"

I admitted I didn't know, but that from what I understood about demon possession, I felt the kind of problems she was describing come about as a result of an outright choice to be on Satan's side. I asked whether the Holy Spirit had convicted her and if she had been unwilling to yield to Him. This she confirmed.

The Exorcist

Many are, no doubt, aware of the film, *The Exorcist*. I understand that it portrays a twelve-year-old girl who plays with a Ouija board and makes a contract with a destructive spirit who causes havoc with human lives. Many people were overwhelmed by fear during and after viewing the picture.

I feel that we must exert care to avoid magnifying the power of Satan rather than emphasizing the love and power of God. Serving God because of this kind of fear is undesirable or meaningless. It is not God's will that man should be the victim of spiritual forces that twist and distort his personality.

The Exorcist is particularly terrifying and dangerous because it vividly describes an encounter with an alien, destructive spirit, but only vaguely indicates how one may be protected from such an influence. We need to emphasize the power that is ours, available to us through Jesus. The power that sustained Him when He walked on earth He will exercise through His servants today.

You don't need to be any particular, special person to pray on behalf of someone in distress, whether spiritual or physical.

If you have a walk with God, if you claim His promises of forgiveness in your own life, and if the victim sincerely desires to be His child, even though weak, then God will work in and through you.

Victory in Christ

I would like to draw your attention to several statements from the writings of Ellen White:

"Angels of God will preserve His people while they walk in the path of duty, but there is no assurance of such protection for those who deliberately venture upon Satan's ground. An agent of the great deceiver will say and do anything to gain his object. . . .

"Could the veil be lifted, we would see evil angels pressing their darkness around us and working with all their power to deceive and destroy."[1]

"Over every soul that is rescued from the power of evil, and whose name is registered in the Lamb's book of life, the controversy is repeated. Never is one received into the family of God without exciting the determined resistance of the enemy. . . .

"His accusations arise solely from his enmity to Christ. . . . All the hatred and malignity of the archrebel is stirred as he beholds the evidences of Christ's supremacy. . . .

"In his own strength, man cannot meet the charges of the enemy. . . .

"Not one soul who in penitence and faith has claimed His protection will Christ permit to pass under the enemy's power. His word is pledged: 'Let him take hold of My strength, that he may make peace with Me; and he shall make peace with Me' (Isaiah 27:5, KJV). The promise given to Joshua is given to all: 'If thou wilt keep My charge, . . . I will give thee places to walk among these that stand by' (Zechariah 3:7, KJV). Angels of God will walk on either side of them, even in this world, and they will stand at last among the angels that surround the throne of God."[2]

Notice the following emphasis on the importance of repentance: "While the followers of Christ have sinned, they have not given themselves up to be controlled by the satanic agencies. They have repented of their sins and have sought the Lord in humility and contrition, and the divine Advocate pleads in their behalf."[3]

References

1. Ellen G. White, *Testimonies for the Church,* Vol. 5, Pacific Press, 1948, page 198, 199.

2. Ellen G. White, *Prophets and Kings*, Pacific Press, 1943, pages 585-587.

3. *Ibid*, p. 589.

Glen G. Gessele, M. Div. is currently pastor of the Hillsboro, Oregon Seventh-day Adventist Church. He and his wife, Marybeth, have two sons.

Deliverance

Deliverance from the control of Satan is deliverance from bondage to sin. This is the essence of salvation. Our understanding of the nature of possession will inevitably influence the way we believe victims of satanic control can be freed. Since the idea of devil possession cannot be clearly understood and presents paradoxes, we must study the whole problem and avoid hastily rejecting any phase merely because it does not appeal to us.

Diagnosis

The cause of mental illness is rarely simple. Damaged brain tissue or abnormal tissue chemistry sometimes accounts for strange behavior. Also, as with a computer, wrong input yields wrong answers. Thus causes of distorted thinking and behavior include physical brain disability and poor thinking habits as well as voluntary submission to satanic control. The intensity of any manifestation of mental disorder is influenced by the individual's intensity of stress and his or her inherent emotional stability. By "emotional stability" we mean the ease with which peace of mind is maintained.

Many cases of demon possession are not obvious, and therefore unrecognized because the individuals appear relatively normal. We cannot say what other unknown or unknowable factors may influence mental illness.

Correct diagnosis requires understanding the disease just as it does for any physical illness. Although not the only cause of disordered thinking, demon possession does disturb the mind.

In the preceding chapter, Pastor Glen Gessele tells about Bob, a young man who experienced periods of demon possessed behavior but who seemed normal at other times. Such a case could be labeled schizophrenic psychosis. Describing mental phenomena like this raises serious questions. Might possession by an unclean spirit be simply a religionist's description of mental illness? Or, from the opposite viewpoint, might psychosis be only a "scientific" term used to deny or conceal Satan's work? Let's consider a blended concept that possession may contribute to psychotic behavior. Thus we can say that a schizophrenic weakness renders certain individuals more susceptible to the temptation to play into the hands of the father of lies.

Personal observation during several decades of medical practice suggests that about 80% of the cost and effort of health care providers in America is expended on problems which could have been avoided. Reliable epidemiologic studies indicate that lifestyle factors, including eating habits, contribute significantly to most cases of severe disability and premature death in the affluent countries of Earth. These observations call our attention to God's rules for healthful living. Respecting these rules leads to health and happiness. Disregarding them leads to disability and disaster.

Thus as a foundation concept in our consideration of possession and mental illness, I believe that ultimately disease and disability are directly or indirectly the result of sin. That is, they result from rebellion against God's natural and/or moral law. (See 1 John 3:4.) Since Satan is the primary leader in rebellion (Revelation 12:7-9), evil spirit possession results from accepting his control and rejecting the direction of the Holy Spirit.

We may not always know whether a person with a mental problem has invited Satan's control, or if so, the depth to which he has surrendered. Nor do we know how much of the dark behavior could be legitimately explained as a mental disease.

But of one thing we can be sure: It is Satan's business to deceive. Thus those who believe they have great knowledge in this area without a firm reliance on the light of God's Word, could certainly be lead to misunderstand–to think distortedly about distorted thinking.

To clarify may I suggest that psychosis is a mental disorder in which personality is seriously disorganized. The perception of reality tends to be distorted, and the ability to think accurately and to reach a logical conclusion is severely impaired.

In a limited way, psychosis is to thinking what limping is to walking. For instance, polio may cause permanent muscle loss or weakness producing a limp. Temporary muscular weakness during recovery from an injury or while a motor nerve is blocked with an anesthetic also causes a limp. Similarly psychosis, or a thinking limp, may result from damaged brain cell connections or from the temporary hypnotizing influence of a controlling spirit. Or it could be caused by a combination of these factors.

In this study, we consider possession to be willful submission to one or the other of two ruling spirits, while recognizing that physical damage also influences behavior. We must never assume that dedicated Christian scholars, physicians or pastors are a part of Satan's deceptive scheme merely because we do not understand their viewpoint.

Causes of mental disturbance are amazingly complex. Psychiatrists and Bible scholars must work in cooperation to understand what God would have us know in order to help people develop God's image mentally as well as physically.

Lloyd and Leola Rosenvold, in their excellent book, *The Battle for the Mind,* write:[1]

". . . psychologists and other mental health scientists who believe that demons exist, in their work and writings attempt to determine the incidence and parameters of what constitutes demonic possession in contradistinction to psychological disease. The present writers will not attempt to enter into such discussions, which too often, even in the hands of learned scientists, end in personal speculations.

"Some neurologists and psychiatrists lean toward the concept that if a medical diagnosis can be applied to a nervous-system derangement then there is not a demonic activity present in that patient. This is not necessarily so. We have already established that whenever there is *any* impairment of the mental functions, Satan can then more easily insinuate himself and gain more and more control over the mind.

"On the other hand, we must guard against the temptation to see a demon behind every stone and stump in the forest and behind every abnormal behavior in a patient. We must also guard against the idea that just because a clinician can justly hang the name of a medical disease on a patient whose symptoms and findings meet the textbook criteria, there could be no demonic overlay present in that patient. Alcoholism is medically considered as a disease. Shall we conclude that because we can identify and name that disease, that there can, therefore, be no demons controlling the thoughts and actions of the inebriate?"

The mind and sanctification

As we consider the many factors which affect the mind, we recall that possession, as God intended it, is alignment of an individual's will with the will of the Holy Spirit. As explained elsewhere in this book, this relationship may be identified with sanctification. Such possession should exist in normal everyday living.

The antithesis of sanctification is alignment of one's will and attitude with the will and attitude of the serpent. This may ultimately become his mark (Rev. 13:16). When fully developed it amounts to permanent rejection of the Holy Spirit (Matt. 12:31). Although we cannot presume to determine any person's eternal destiny, we sometimes meet individuals who seem able to clearly differentiate right from wrong, yet who deliberately choose the wrong whenever it pleases them. They simply do not seem to care. Some of these may be fully possessed by an evil spirit, or a combination of factors may exist.

Do you remember the story of Judas at the Passover supper? "When the Saviour's hands were bathing those soiled feet, and wiping them with the towel, the heart of Judas thrilled . . . with the impulse . . . to confess his sin. But he would not humble himself. He hardened his heart against repentance. . . . He was possessed by a demon, and he resolved to complete the work he had agreed to do."[2]

As we have already pointed out, possession may vary from being barely perceptible on the one hand, to a state of greatly altered awareness, bizarre behavior, and perhaps abnormal muscular tension on the other. Such intense manifestation of possession by the Holy Spirit rarely occurs even during inspired vision. On the other hand, intense satanic possession is not rare. It is seen in voodoo worship and other forms of demon possession. It also occurs during a spiritualistic medium's seance. A similar state may be induced by a hypnotist or it may be simulated by hysterical response to overwhelming stress.

The would-be exorcist should understand the complex possibilities. The desire of the troubled individual to accept divine control may be difficult to assess, but without this personal determination, genuine success cannot be achieved.

Treatment

Efforts to relieve demon possession often focus on spectacular manifestations. To avoid embarrassing the cause of Christ and to really benefit the afflicted individual, each case must be carefully and prayerfully studied.[3] It would also be well to consult with persons experienced in the study and treatment of mental disease, and with those whom God has ordained to lead out in spiritual matters.

"It is the nicest [most delicate] and most critical . . . work ever given to mortals, to deal with minds. Those who engage in this work should have clear discernment and good powers of discrimination."[4]

"When . . . [the God-fearing physician] has gained the confidence of the afflicted by relieving their sufferings and bringing them back from the verge of the grave he may teach them that disease is the result of sin and that it is the fallen foe who seeks to allure them to the health-and-soul-destroying practices. He may impress their minds with the necessity of denying self and obeying the laws of life and health."[5]

The chapter, "Mind Cure," in the book, *The Ministry of Healing*,[6] outlines valuable principles for the treatment of diseased minds. Unfortunately such treatment is costly in terms of loving professional time. Many patients needing such care are financially impoverished by the time they seek or are brought for help. However, to ignore these principles and depend entirely on medication as a substitute for the more demanding "natural remedies" offers less than ideal patient care.

An improved lifestyle is important in achieving lasting results. But, although it must be sincerely recommended, only the sick person can accept and implement it. At the same time, even when the natural help is accepted, some symptoms may still need to be relieved by medication.

Dangers of the deliverance ministry

Caution is in order. Exorcism frequently tends to be a spectacular exhibition. But the exorcist must not presume to command the Holy Spirit to heal sickness or to miraculously displace an evil spirit. Otherwise exorcism sessions may resemble certain "charismatic" exercises where the miracle worker attempts to make God his servant drawing attention to his own supposed power! The exorcist thus plays into the hands of Satan who releases his depressing influence on cue to produce "healing." As a result both the exorcist and the tormented one are brought under demonic influence.

As time progresses, we expect Satan's miracle-working activity to increase (Rev. 13:11-14). For this reason we dare not accept miracles as conclusive evidence that God is at work.

Repeating magic words, even though they may contain the name of God, is not the province of a person dealing with the problem of possession. Scripture forbids communication with evil spirits (Deut. 18:9-24). Exorcists who dialogue with demons ignore this warning. The victim must desire not merely relief but a different master. He or she must be willing to accept Jesus as Lord. The Holy Spirit will not impose Himself on anyone. Our major role is to lift up the Saviour and to intercede. Every release from the slavery of sin is a miracle.

We serve a miracle-working God. He feeds the hungry and clothes the naked, and He expects us to participate by using every means He has placed in our hands. This principle applies whether the disorder is physical in origin or spirit induced.

God's promises are conditional. For instance, "I will do whatever you ask in my name, *so that the Father may be glorified in the Son*" (John 14:13, emphasis supplied). Directly related to the problem we are discussing, are these words: "God did extraordinary miracles through Paul . . . their diseases left them, and the evil spirits came out of them. Then some itinerant Jewish exorcists tried to use the name of the Lord Jesus over those who had evil spirits, saying, 'I adjure you by the Jesus whom Paul proclaims.'" (Acts 19:11-13). Their attempt failed.

Commenting on this experience, Ellen White wrote, "The apostles were not always able to work miracles at will. The Lord granted His servants this special power as the progress of His cause or the honor of His name required."[7]

The Rosenvolds broadly discuss the deliverance ministry,

commenting on how the evil one so often uses it as a game to deceive both the exorcist and the one supposedly delivered. They point out that ". . . many mental and emotional disturbances are the consequence of the patient having in one way or another yielded to Satan's allurements to sin, thereby coming under his control."[8] Victory comes, not by dramatic ceremony, but by change in the character worked out day by day in the power of the Holy Spirit.[9]

Efforts to lead those under Satan's power to find deliverance should yield dramatic results for individuals who are able to choose and who sincerely want to surrender their hearts to the rule of the Holy Spirit. Failure occurs in those who are unable or unwilling to make such a choice. The behavior of those who are released from demon possession depends on the extent of physical derangement in their brain structure and on their commitment to the Holy Spirit's control.

References

1. Lloyd and Leola Rosenvold, *The Battle for the Mind,* pp. 79, 80. Hope International, Eatonville, Washington. 1979.

2. Ellen G. White, *The Desire of Ages,* p. 645. Pacific Press. Nampa, Idaho, 1898, 1940. Also John 13:27.

3. Lyndon K. McDowell, "Demons and Deliverance," *Ministry,* April, 1987. pp. 4-7.

4. Ellen G. White, *Testimonies for the Church,* Vol. 3, p. 104. Pacific Press, 1948.

5. Ellen G. White, Testimonies for the Church, Vol. 5, pp. 444, 445.

6. Ellen G. White, *The Ministry of Healing.* Pacific Press, 1905, 1942.

7. Ellen G. White, *Seventh-day Adventist Bible Commentary,* Vol. 6, p. 1064. Review and Herald. Hagerstown, Maryland, 1957.

8. Rosenvold, *Op. Cit.,* p. 5.

9. Rosenvold, *Op. Cit.,* pp. 32-35.

In the Church

By Pastor Rick Howard

Spiritualism, like an ancient monster, masquerades in curious forms as it appears from generation to generation. It entices its victims through the allurements of hidden knowledge and mystical power. Spiritualism was practiced under the direction of ancient astrologers and sun-worshiping Egyptian priests, and through the witchcraft of the Medieval Age.

Today, in a variety of disguises, it extends its appeal to practically all levels and groups of society. Excitement seekers turn to the Ouija board. The bereaved seek spirit mediums. Men looking for friendship and power are drawn into Secret Societies. New Age teachings appeal to humanistic intellectuals and others looking for a better world. And some, with confidence in their primitive roots, are drawn by voodoo worship and witch doctors.

In whatever face this monster appears, mystical knowledge and power are the baits dangled before its intended victims. These same enticements tempted our first parents in Eden, and ever since have led souls down paths to loss of control of the will, our most important faculty.

Evil angels in control
Ellen White writes of evil angels controlling minds. She noted that "Spiritualism is about to take the world captive,"[1] and that "few have any idea as to what will be the manifestations of spiritualism in the future."[2]

In 1875 she predicted: "These manifestations will be more frequent, and developments of a more startling character will appear as we near the close of time."[3]

For years traditional Christian practices have been leaning ever so gently toward Eastern mystical traditions, advancing quietly enough to avoid fear in most Christian circles. The "mind science" movements labeled EST or scientology, positive or possibility thinking, and positive confession share a common philosophy. They build on the idea that all is governed by a higher law or force located within the mind and controlled with positive thinking and meditative techniques. Norman Vincent Peale and Robert Schuller have been advocating such theories for years.

According to Pastor C. S. Lovett,[4] by access to one's unconscious mind, a person could command the healing of any disease. He believes Jesus healed that way and assumes we should be able to tap the same tremendous power. Thus, basic spiritualistic philosophy of 50 years ago is now considered Christian by many ministers.

The popular book, *The Seduction of Christianity*, emphasizes the alarming extent to which these practices, under philosophical labels, are entering the Christian churches.[5] And Ellen White warns, "As spiritualism more closely imitates the nominal Christianity of the day, it has greater power to deceive and ensnare."[6]

Many who seek spiritual fulfillment through the concepts and meditative practices of Eastern religions don't know that these are simply ancient methods of mind possession.

Visualization

Meditation in all forms of spiritualistic practices from ancient witchcraft to modern Eastern and Western mysticism are bound by the common thread of visualization or mental imagery. Occult science secrets based on mystical experiences" are revealed in the writings of Western mystics like Henry David Thoreau and Walt Whitman, as well in as those of Eastern Hindu gurus such as Sri Chinmoy (spiritual leader of the United Nations) or Maharishi Mahesh Yogi.

Occultist, David Conway, explains the importance of visualization in occult phenomena: "The technique of visualization is something you will gradually master, and indeed must master if you are to make any progress at all in magic. . . . It is our only means of affecting the etheric atmosphere.

"It enables us to build our own thought forms, contact those already in existence and channel the elemental energy we need onto the physical plane."[7]

The terms "thought forms" and "elemental energy" refer to trance experiences of those who have attained altered states of consciousness. In these altered states, thoughts are perceived to have structure. By intense concentration, they actually become reality to the participant.

The corridor

Students of mystical sciences soon learn about a definite mental corridor between the conscious and the subconscious through which supernatural experiences flow. In this corridor of the mind the spirit medium communicates with the so-called spirits of the dead, the occultist supposedly leaves his body in astral projection, and the psychic sees visions of the future. And the hypnotist draws his subject here to manipulate the subconscious.

The great deceiver has also packaged ways to enter this communication corridor for sale to the church. For over a thousand years mystics with the Christian name have been wilfully entering this state of mind seeking visionary experiences.

Thoughts naturally flit across the mind, and considering an idea generally brings up related thoughts. Occultists teach that, by visualization and concentration, this natural flow of thoughts can be interrupted. As this occurs, subjects slip into an altered state of consciousness which we have identified as the corridor of the mind.

To the Hindu this state is "illumination." To the Buddhist, it is "enlightenment." The hypnotist or spirit medium understands it as a "trance." And the psychic or trance channeler might call it "tuning in."

Ellen White labeled the practices that produce these experiences as hypnotism or mesmerism. While the experimenter believes to have reached a place of power within, control of the mind has actually been relinquished to a power without!

Visualization is not the only means of altering consciousness. Drugs such as marijuana, LSD, or other hallucinogens can specifically alter the thought rate placing it in that supernatural corridor.[8]

Seeking spiritual growth by altered consciousness

Any type of concentration on sensual stimulation may alter consciousness. Music with a strong rhythm, or concentration on the relaxation of different parts of the body, can induce it. The apparently innocent concentration on a mental image of Jesus standing in your favorite spot can bring the same effect.

Altering consciousness by any method can be used to wilfully contact the supernatural world. Or, even without specific invitation, the supernatural forces can use them to contact those who practice them. Thus evil powers have easy access to minds placed in such a condition. The serpent, cast out of heaven, is still battling God for the control of human minds.

"For our struggle is not against enemies of blood and flesh, but against the rulers, against the authorities, against the cosmic powers of this present darkness, against the spiritual forces of evil in the heavenly places" (Eph. 6:12).

Many who consider the traditional Christian worship to be

dull, turn easily to mystical experiences. Korean Pastor Paul Yonggi Cho responds to this interest. He teaches that God used imagination in creating the world, and that "men (Christian or Occultist,) by exploring their spiritual sphere of the fourth dimension through the development of concentrated visions and dreams in their imaginations, can brood over and incubate the third dimension, influencing and changing it."[9] He says that the Holy Spirit taught him this, but the idea is related to the Hindu concept of being like God in reproducing reality with the semiconscious mind.

Thus the supernatural demonstrations that began with the talking serpent in Eden are more and more infecting Christian worship.

Guided meditation

Ancient occult mind science has tiptoed into God's church dressed as modern psychology. It tells us we may create by visualizing our desires. In well-meaning efforts to improve their spiritual condition, many have embraced practices of mind control without considering that none of these methods has any scriptural foundation. In seminars across the country, church leaders and pastors are learning the mental disciplines of "guided meditation" and "visualization."

Guided meditation is similar to the nineteenth-century "mind-cure" techniques of hypnotism. Ellen White wrote: "We do not ask you to place yourself under the control of any man's mind. The mind cure is the most awful science which has ever been advocated. Every wicked being can use it in carrying through his own evil designs. We have no business with any such science. We should be afraid of it. Never should the first principles of it be brought into any institution."[10]

In guided meditations, people activate a power that enables them to focus the mind's eye through suggestions of another person. This appears innocent because visualizing is a normal part of reading or listening. But the danger is that *the concentrated effort to sustain mental pictures is the key that unlocks the door to altered states of consciousness.*

In essence mind cure pretends to heal through controlled imagination. The sick body is visualized in a healthy condition through the essential techniques of hypnosis. Psychic healers, advocates of mind control, and modern Christian healers all operate this way.

Scripture demonstrates that God has always taken the initiative when supernatural communication with man was necessary. Visions and dreams were given to His agents when God saw fit.[12] Altered states of consciousness occurred often during these supernatural revelations. But we have no evidence whatsoever that any Bible prophet ever practiced mind manipulation seeking a different level of consciousness. They prayed as you or I would, and God responded appropriately. In fact the Scriptures warn repeatedly against spiritualistic philosophies:

"Do not let anyone disqualify you, insisting on self-abasement and worship of angels, dwelling on visions, puffed up without cause by way of a human way of thinking" (Col. 2:18).

The easy way

Meditation techniques are not justified by combining Scripture "guidance" with them. Satan is obviously pleased by the self-confidence of Bible students who try to make their own channel of communication. He stands at the other end to give deception the sound of truth. We may invite the Holy Spirit's guidance knowing that He appeals in the still, small voice to the free mind.

Many, possibly through curiosity or a lack of commitment to intense Bible study, search for easier spiritual experiences. Through ecstatic feelings they achieve a deceptive sense of peace. Thus what were once considered isolated false

Christian practices have become new ways to worship in increasing numbers of congregations. Satan is seeking to put people to sleep in the final hours of probation.

Let's remember that "The secret things belong to the Lord our God, but the revealed things belong to us and to our children forever" (Deut. 29:29). ". . . come out from them, and be separate from them, says the Lord, and touch nothing unclean; then I will welcome you, and I will be your father, and you shall be my sons and daughters, says the Lord Almighty" (2 Cor. 6:17).

References

1. Ellen G. White, Undated manuscript 66.

2. *Ibid.*

3. Ellen G. White, *Evangelism*, p. 604.

4. C. S. Lovett, "The Medicine of Your Mind," *Personal Christianity Newsletter*, August 1979.

5. Dave Hunt and T. A. McMahon, *Op cit.*

6. Ellen G. White, *The Great Controversy, Op. cit.*

7. David Conway, *Magic: An Occult Primer.*

8. See Charles T. Tart, *Altered States of Consciousness*, p. 416. John Wiley and Sons, 1969.

9. Paul Yonggi Cho, *Fourth*, pp. 39-44. As quoted by Hunt and McMahon, *Op. cit.* Pastor Cho is an evangelical pastor in Korea whose congregation numbers in the tens of thousands.

10. Ellen G. White, *Medical Ministry*, p. 116. Also see her statements in *Medical Ministry*, pp. 110, 111; *Selected Messages*, Book 2, pp. 350, 351.

Before committing his life to Christ, Rick Howard was deep into many of the practices he discusses. As this book is published, he is pastor of the New England Memorial Seventh-day Adventist Church. He praises God for granting his escape from Satan's hold over those who tamper with his power. An article similar to this chapter appeared as "Mysticism in the Church," in *Our Firm Foundations*. (Eatonville, WA).

Will and salvation

Will is the capacity of conscious and deliberate choice and action. In the will lies the power of self-direction. It distinguishes a free person. As Ellen White puts it, "The will is the governing power in the nature of man, bringing all other faculties under its sway. The will is not the taste or the inclination, but it is the deciding power which works in the children of men unto obedience to God or unto disobedience."[1] This chapter shows that the right use of the will is crucial in salvation, because virtually every facet of moral responsibility involves this function. Earlier in this book, we observed that hypnotism controls one's concept of reality and the ability to recognize truth and falsehood.

As we have seen, a hypnotist's influence on his subject seems to be similar to that exerted by a supernatural spirit on a possessed person. Also, submission to either the Holy Spirit or an evil spirit is by free choice. But in the case of evil spirit possession, a person has little or no control after the choice is made. Similarly, the hypnotized subject, after choosing to submit, has little, if any, control of the fully developed process. Suggestions accepted during a trance may persist after release. And some people may be more vulnerable to subsequent domination after repeated hypnotic experiences.

Therefore, the warnings of Ellen White concerning the dangers of "mesmerism" are not to be taken lightly. The correct exercise of the will and power of discrimination are, obviously, directly related to the prospect of enjoying life in the new earth.

As repeatedly pointed out, not only is the process of

awareness distorted during hypnosis, but the very important function of will is surrendered to the hypnotist, and with it the ability to discriminate and choose are relinquished. The importance of free, responsible exercise of the will becomes even clearer as we explore its relation to the many facets of salvation.

Perfect will

Let's consider the implication of Jesus' advice, "Be perfect, therefore, as your heavenly Father is perfect" (Matt. 5:48). I believe He is speaking of the completeness of our trust. We must be willing to be His people. We must allow Him to be our only God because loyalty cannot be divided. Jesus' love for us is perfect with no taint of insincerity. Therefore He rightfully expects our whole-hearted cooperation as our will blends into complete harmony with His. As our characters are thus transformed, we experience the joy of His peace.

God never forces His way on anyone. Those who accept Him believe that He loves them personally and that He will ask only what is ultimately best for them. They believe that His advice really works and are willing to follow His way of life. From this we get a faint glimpse of how God's image is restored in us and what it means to be perfect.

Will and eternal life

In a government based on unrestricted freedom and genuine love, everyone's will and purpose must be in complete harmony. This is what makes the everlasting covenant work. If selfishness, greed or jealousy taint any individual's will, the freedom of all is destroyed.

"I seek to do not my own will," Jesus said, "but the will of him who sent me." (John 5:30). And in finally accepting death for our sins, He declared, "not my will, but yours, be done" (Luke 22:42). Jesus told Nicodemus, "no one can see the kingdom of God without being born from above" (John

3.3). And so He invites us to make a fresh start—to have our wills washed clean by His Spirit.

Will is paramount. In fact, it appears that whoever is willing to go will be taken to heaven. For instance, "whosoever will, let him take the water of life freely" (Rev. 22:17, KJV). Of course, the offer is not for some who might like to go along just for the ride. It does include everyone who is *willing* to live by the rules which make happy existence possible. Personal choice determines in each case whether salvation is possible.

With freedom comes responsibility. Every free person is responsible for his or her willingness or unwillingness to accept God's offers of mercy.

Ellen White has written, "We are to live in conformity to His will, representing Him in life and character. Perfect conformity to the will of God is the condition of which eternal life is given. . . . May the Lord bless you, my brother and sister, and lead you, through a knowledge of His Word, to a perfect understanding of His will concerning you."[2]

Words such as sin, justification, sanctification and salvation become more meaningful by viewing the will as their common denominator. Instead of independent religious ideas, they become aspects of the very same important relationship between our Creator and His free creatures.

Law

Natural law is a compact description of the of events which occur consistently under identical circumstances. Natural law exists because of the dependable nature of the Creator. Laws, such as the law of gravitation, have existed since creation but remain unrecognized until they are discovered by careful observation.

In a parallel way, God's moral law is actually a compact description of the lifestyle which He recommends knowing that it leads to happiness. The law warns that an opposite course would result in sorrow and disaster. His ability to foresee the inevitable result of every course of action which man might choose assures the absolute accuracy of His recommendations. Our desire to conform to this law is influenced by how much we trust its Author. Choosing to obey means exercising the will.

Sin

Sin is "lawlessness" (1 John 3:4). In other words, sin is willful contempt for the principles of righteousness and deliberate disregard of warnings of its consequences. Sin is rebellion, and rebellion is basically an attitude of the will. Elimination of sin requires a reversal of this attitude — a realignment of the will.

Atonement

Unity is emphasized in Jesus' prayer, "that they may be one even as we are one, I in them and you in me, that they may become completely one, so that the world may know that you have sent me" (John 17:22, 23). This prayer is the key to understanding the atonement.

Atonement describes the restoration of genuine unity among God's children, and between Him and His people. Rumor suggests that an early translator of the Bible was unable to find an English word which he felt accurately conveyed the meaning of God's act of restoration. Therefore, he coined the word at-one-ment which has become "atonement" in our day.

Atonement is a two-phase process. The first was establishing God's credibility before all the universe, and revealing Lucifer's hateful character. This phase of atonement Jesus completed when He lived and died on earth, welding the loyalty of unfallen beings to Himself. The second phase produces the necessary change in attitude in the heart of every redeemed slave—a change from rebellion to trust. Actually, atonement is realigning the will of the once estranged creature into harmony with the will of the Creator. This is reconciliation.

"If we consent, He will so identify Himself with our thoughts and aims, so blend our hearts and minds into conformity to His will, that when obeying Him we shall be but carrying out our own impulses. The will, refined and sanctified, will find its highest delight in doing His service. When we know God as it is our privilege to know Him, our life will be a life of continual obedience."[3]

In other words, when my will is so blended with His will that in serving Him I am simply carrying out the desire of my own heart, then I have become one with Him. My atonement has been accomplished.

Sanctification

"True sanctification is an entire conformity to the will of God."[4] Without a free, discriminating will there can be no sanctified life.

Justification

"As the penitent sinner, contrite before God, discerns Christ's atonement in his behalf, and accepts this atonement as his only hope in this life and the future life, his sins are pardoned. This is justification by faith."[5]

Salvation

Accepting the atonement—God's gift of reconciliation—requires discernment, discrimination and action of the will. It means choosing to be totally possessed by the Holy Spirit.

From all this we see that salvation is impossible without atonement—without realignment of our perverse human will and objectives to be in harmony with God's will. Also, accepting atonement—God's gift of reconciliation—and choosing to comply with the conditions which must accompany it require discernment, unimpaired discrimination and action of the will. We cannot afford to participate in any experience which might compromise this.

References

1. Ellen G. White, *Testimonies for the Church,* Vol. 5, p. 513. Pacific Press. Nampa, Idaho, 1948.

2. Ellen G. White, *This Day With God,* p. 372. Review and Herald. Hagerstown, Maryland, 1979.

3. Ellen G. White, *The Desire of Ages,* p. 668. Pacific Press. 1940.

4. Ellen G. White, *Sanctified Life,* p. 9. Review and Herald. 1937.

5. Ellen G. White, *Seventh-day Adventist Bible Commentary,* p. 1070. Review and Herald. 1957.

Conquering

To conquer means to overcome, to gain possession or control by physical, mental or moral force. Conquering requires the action of vigorous, unhampered will.

In other terms, conquering implies a conflict resulting in victory. It is not the result of wishful thinking, but requires dedicated effort. It takes the perseverance of a vigorous will. And it requires discrimination—knowing which voice to obey.

Eternal rewards are promised those who emerge victorious. They will eat of the tree of life, escape the second death, receive a new name, receive power, and have their names retained in the book of life. (Rev. 2:7, 11, 17, 26; 3:5).

In view of these promises, the following admonition is well worth heeding. "Therefore . . . let us also lay aside every weight . . . and let us run with perseverance the race . . . looking unto Jesus . . . who . . . endured the cross, disregarding the shame and has taken his seat at the right hand of the throne of God" (Heb. 12:1, 2).

At this point, we seem to be confronted by a paradox. In the previous chapter we saw the importance of surrendering the will to God. Can surrender mean victory? This seems impossible.

Surrender to Christ is freedom

Someone could say, "What I don't understand about Christianity is the idea that I am free and at the same time always required to submit my will to Christ." This touches the very heart of the Gospel and the truth about the character of God. Let's take a closer look.

If God were making rules strictly to suit His own

convenience or whim, the idea would be preposterous. It would be an exchange of one kind of slavery for another. However, God is absolutely fair. He practices the golden rule Himself. And He is infinitely wise. His rules point out the best way. A person who has faith in God's love, mercy and wisdom, views divine law as prophecy showing the outcome of various possible ways of life.

God did not stumble along, trying one behavior and then another to see which would work. He has the capacity to know the end result from the beginning. Since we trust God, we trust His rules.

The Bible teaches that each individual is responsible for his or her actions. We must all weigh each alternative in the light of God's advice, and choose the right. Thus we obey God by conscious choice and not blindly. We are always free to disobey. On the other hand, force and coercion are Satan's methods and were never condoned by Christ. Christianity, rightly practiced, strengthens the will. The Christian aligned with Christ is the freest of all people, because he has joined his will to God's will as a voluntary act. When I become a Christian, it is not the result of being overpowered or subdued. I chose to form a partnership with One whose purpose is to help me. Happiness, peace and joy in the kingdom of heaven require intelligent, voluntary cooperation.

Surrender to the will of God is not a passive experience. It is neither following the path of least resistance nor is it being pushed around as by a bully.

Alignment of my will with His requires willingness to follow His plan and to accept His advice even when it crosses my natural inclination. It requires total commitment. The power of the will increases with use—by making firm decisions. It is increased by rapport with the will of the Holy Spirit.

Our Redeemer cannot stamp His seal of approval on any lukewarm, half-hearted follower. "Christ, the heavenly merchantman seeking goodly pearls, saw in lost humanity the pearl of [great] price. . . . God looked upon humanity, not as vile and worthless . . . . He collected all the riches of the universe, and laid them down in order to buy the pearl."[1] Christ gave Himself completely, that He might forgive our sins. Therefore, it is reasonable that He should expect us to give ourselves completely.

Hypnosis and conquering

The foregoing comments imply relationships between domination and hypnosis on the one hand, and will and conquering on the other. That is, how can surrender lead to bondage in the case of hypnotism, and to freedom in God's plan for life?

To creatures made in His image, God grants freedom that they may serve with loyalty based on appreciation of His character. Freedom implies the unimpaired right to choose one's course of action. Freedom to choose bondage and to sincerely believe falsehood. The free individual is accountable not only for his acts but for the choices leading to those acts. Choice is an act of the will. Intelligent choice requires discrimination. Both will and discrimination are surrendered during hypnosis. How quickly they are regained is uncertain.

Surrender of self to Christ prepares a person for being filled with the Holy Spirit—for yielding to the Spirit's influence. As we compare this experience with surrender during hypnotic trance, we see both similarity and contrast. Complete submission is required in each case. The cooperation God expects is always a voluntary response in a love relationship. By contrast, while hypnotized one does not choose to obey or exercise the will. Instead, he is as though he had no will at all. In fact, to ponder and deliberate prevents participation in the trance state. The hypnotized person acts out the hypnotist's suggestions without regard for his own inclinations. His obedience becomes more unquestioning as the trance deepens.

It is difficult to imagine a surrender of the will more total than that which requires a person to believe something is true when his senses would plainly declare it false.

Because obedience is not easy in a sinful world, the Christian's will must be unimpaired. He must choose and act. More than that, the effectiveness of the human will depends on its ability to resonate with God's will. A vibrating string by itself produces an unimpressive sound. But when this string is mounted on a good violin and under the bow of a master violinist, it can fill an auditorium with delightful sound. So it is when our human will is voluntarily joined by faith to the divine will. The result is harmony and victory.

Notice how Ellen White explains it: "The will must be brought into complete harmony with the will of God. When this is done, no ray of light that shines into the heart and chambers of the mind will be resisted . . . . The light from heaven is welcomed, as light filling all the chambers of the soul. This is making melody to God."[2]

"The soul that is yielded to Christ, becomes His own fortress which He holds in a revolted world, and he intends that no authority shall be known in it but His own. A soul thus kept in possession by the heavenly agencies, is impregnable to the assaults of Satan. But unless we do yield ourselves to the control of Christ, we shall be dominated by the wicked one. We must inevitably be under the control of the one or the other of the two great powers that are contending for the supremacy of the world."[3]

The same personal control of the will which is exercised for conquering in the day-to-day battles of life is also essential for victory in confrontation with supernatural forces of deception. We next consider the spectacular event which we have been warned will occur before Christ returns.

References

1. Ellen G. White, *Christ's Object Lessons,* p. 118. Pacific Press. Nampa, Idaho, 1900.

2. Ellen G. White *Review and Herald,* Feb. 24, 1977.

3. Ellen G. White *The Desire of Ages,* p. 324. Pacific Press. 1898. New York, 1951.

Impending deception

Jesus told us that just before His return, "false messiahs . . . will appear and produce great signs and omens to lead astray. . . ." (Matt. 24:24). And in Ellen White's book, *The Great Controversy*, we read: "As the crowning act in the great drama of deception, Satan himself will personate Christ. . . . The great deceiver will make it appear that Christ has come. In different parts of the earth, Satan will manifest himself . . . as a majestic being of dazzling brightness . . . . His voice is soft and subdued, yet full of melody. . . . This is the strong, almost overmastering delusion.   Like the Samaritans who were deceived by Simon Magnus, the multitudes, from the least to the greatest, give heed to these sorceries."[1] Sorcery is the use of a supernatural or evil power over people or their affairs.

We may add to this another thought to fill out the picture: Satan "will exercise his power and work upon the human imagination. He will corrupt both the minds and the bodies of men, and will work through the children of disobedience, fascinating and charming, as does a serpent. . . .

"The form Satan assumed in Eden when leading our first parents to transgress, was of a character to bewilder and confuse the mind. He will work in as subtle a manner as we near the end of earth's history. All his deceiving power will be brought to bear upon human subjects, to complete the work of deluding the human family."[2]

It is more than interesting to notice how Bernheim uses the word fascination. "Fascination . . . is always hypnosis, that is to say, an exalted susceptibility to suggestion induced by an influence exercised over the subject's imagination."[3]

From their study of the subtle influences in the modern Christian church, Hunt and McMahon conclude that:

"There can be little doubt that we are in the midst of an unprecedented revival of sorcery worldwide that is deeply affecting not only every level and sector of modern society, but the church as well. Known as the New Age, Holistic, Human Potential, or Consciousness movements, at its heart is what anthropologists now call shamanism, which is simply the old occultism made to sound native, natural, earthy, and thus wholesome. It is also made to sound Christian. We have attempted [in the book, *The Seduction of Christianity*,] to present an understanding of the various ways under which the same delusion that is preparing the world for the Antichrist is now seducing Christianity itself.

"It has been our concern to document the fact that the seduction is already upon us, and that not only in the secular world, but within the church as well, what is happening seems to fit the very pattern prophesied for the period of time just before the return of Christ for His own. It should be clear that what we are facing is not merely a pocket of questionable teaching here and there, but a rapidly spreading acceptance of ideas within the church that represent a revival of ancient occultism and can be traced back to the lie of the Serpent in the Garden of Eden."[4]

Seventh-day Adventists have long anticipated the amalgamation of religions.[5] Hunt and McMahon report the shaping of just such a movement in the world around us on a grander scale than we could ever have imagined. Of particular interest to our study is their idea that spirit possession and sorcery are at the very heart of the image to the beast (Rev. 13:14, 15).

A mental picture

Have you tried to picture in your mind the powerful delusion calculated to lead astray the very elect? (Matt.

24:23-26). Evangelist George Vandeman points out that "Satan's obsession with getting the worship of men will culminate in his impersonating Christ himself."[6] Spirit possession and hypnosis will no doubt contribute to such a phenomenon.

An experience reported by B. C. Gindes demonstrates how hypnosis can alter awareness: ". . . a college student was told under hypnosis that she would see her brother (who had been dead for two years!), six months later, at 11:00 AM on a specific date. At precisely the appointed time, she was astounded to 'meet' her brother on a street in Los Angeles. These were her words: 'I was so happy to see him, but I was astonished because I knew he was dead . . . . He accompanied me to my apartment, and there we talked about different things . . . . Soon he arose from his chair with the excuse that he had to keep an appointment, and left . . . [I was bewildered] until it was explained to me that my illusion was part of an hypnotic experiment.'"[7]

It is unimportant whether we recognize this as hypnosis or as spirit manifestation similar to that performed by the medium at Endor (1 Samuel 28:3-14). The ultimate controlling power is the same in either case.

Observe that in our day many people are being conditioned by spiritism, rock music, glossolalia and similar forms of ecstatic experience. As you think of this, remember that frequent repetition of any form of possession or hypnosis may increase the ease of repetition. Also consider the prevalence of the false assumption that miraculous events and experiences indicate that God Himself must be at work. Thus we find a combination of factors which have the potential of producing dramatic distortion of awareness.

Although we don't know exactly how this widespread participation in trance-like experiences could contribute to the world's great final deception, the following scenario seems plausible to me:

Picture in the foreground a restless throng. Here are people almost desperate from the tension caused by increasing troubles on every side. They have assembled for worship, and are longing for relief. Now their fervor is being intensified by peaceless, loud, soul-jarring, quasi-religious music. Exuding charisma, their leader "heals" a few lame ones. Here and there ecstatic prayers and speeches are heard. Gradually a hypnoid trance pervades the group. Then suddenly, the leader turns with a sweeping gesture and cries, "Jesus, Jesus!" Ecstasy prevails as a beautiful being appears in dazzling splendor. He moves gracefully. He raises his arms to quiet the cheering throng. He speaks words of peace and joy with a rich, full voice. He assures them that by trusting him none will be lost. They have no need to worry about anything they may do because they believe he has covered their sins at the cross.

This occurs at many places in large and small gatherings. But even those unable to join the crowds are not forgotten. Imagine a lonely figure who has achieved ecstasy in solitude and who supposes that such a feeling can be only of divine origin. A bright being also appears to this isolated one with the same message. Anticipation is rewarded. The deception is accepted.

Thus masses of humanity are turned away from the real Jesus. Those who do not guard and exercise their ability to conquer, will in the end, be conquered by the evil one.

References

1. Ellen G. White, *The Great Controversy,* pp. 624, 625. Pacific Press. 1911. Also compare *Testimonies for the Church,* Vol. 5, pp. 293, 294 by the same author. Pacific Press. 1948.

2. Ellen G. White, *Seventh-day Adventist Bible Commentary,* Vol. 5, p. 1106. Review and Herald. Hagerstown, Maryland, 1956.

3. H. Bernheim, *Hypnosis and Suggestion,* p. 17. (Trans. from 2nd

rev. ed. by Christian Herter). University Books. New Hyde Park, New York, 1964.

4. Dave Hunt and T. A. McMahon, *Op. Cit.,* p. 213.

5. Ellen G. White, *Testimonies to the Church,* vol. 5, pp. 454; and *The Great Controversy,* pp. 588, 589.

6. George E. Vandeman, "The Great Impersonation," *Channels,* Fall, 1986, p. 12.

7. B. C. Gindes, *New Concepts of Hypnosis,* p. 39, 40. Copyright 1951 by Bernard C. Gindes, M.D. Renewed © 1979 by Hanna E. Gindes. Used by permission of The Julian Press, Inc. New York.

The choice is ours

The Creator endowed each of us with ability to reason, to discriminate, to love and to be loyal. These gifts may be perfected in Christ, or they may be distorted by rebellion resulting in ultimate self-destruction. Our eternal destiny depends on how we use and cherish them.

The infinite mind of God is able to consider and resolve innumerable problems simultaneously. But we humans have been provided with an awareness selection mechanism which permits our small minds to avoid confusion by being able to carefully consider only one thing at a time. This mechanism is subject to manipulation and distortion.

Furthermore, God has provided a way for us to communicate with the Holy Spirit. In a way that is not entirely clear, manipulation of this mechanism is related to hypnosis and to evil spirit possession.

Awareness of our physical and emotional environment is normal. As gregarious individuals, suggestions of associates rightfully influence us. Hypnotic suggestion, however, is abnormal. It distorts awareness and obliterates discrimination.

A sense of God's majesty and glory naturally thrill us with excitement and awe. But only through self-control in Christ may we be safe from deception. As we prepare for the return of our Lord, we must be alert to recognize counterfeit ecstatic experiences which often wear the cloak of religion. Supernatural spirits of one kind or another do influence our minds. It is our responsibility to choose which ones.

"Here is a call for the endurance of the saints, those who keep the commandments of God and hold fast to the faith of Jesus" (Rev. 14:12).

Theodore E. Wade, M.D., M.S., F.A.C.S., has studied the process and dangers of hypnotism and similar phenomena for many years. He was born in 1904, and he grew up in Cañon City, Colorado. He graduated from Union College and from The College of Medical Evangelists (now Loma Linda University). He has practiced general medicine and surgery in Colorado, California, and Kansas. During the Second World War, he served with the U.S. military. As this book is published, he lives in retirement with his wife, Zola, in Liberal, Kansas.